GW01046780

Romany Boy

Romany Boy

Leon Petulengro

ROBERT HALE · LONDON

ISBN 0 7091 7864 6

Robert Hale Limited
Clerkenwell House
Clerkenwell Green
London, EC1R 0HT

Printed in Great Britain by
Lowe & Brydone Printers Limited, Thetford, Norfolk
Photoset by Rowland Phototypesetting Limited,
Bury St. Edmunds, Suffolk

Contents

Illustrations

PICTURE CREDITS
   Syndication International Ltd   1, 6, 7, 8, 9, 10, 11
   Andrew Jones   2, 3, 4

To
my mother

1

Early Memories

My first memory is of waking on a June day to see my father's face—large, mustachioed, dark, and round like a full moon which temporarily eclipsed the sunlight filtering through the leaves whispering above my head.

I stared upwards, clinging to the edge of sleep, aware of the soft, warm flank of the grey donkey on which my head rested, its damp, gentle smell, the surprised whistle of a starling, the silky texture of an afternoon breeze; and a swift flutter of happiness stirred in me before he spoke.

"Caught you. Having a kip, eh?" His voice rumbled deep in his broad chest like a sleeping volcano. "Lazy-bones, the both of you." His chuckle was rich as he took my hand. "Come along, Lion. Your mother had been wondering where you are." (Lion was his name for me.)

I staggered up and pulled at the donkey's head—my pet, companion, friend. My father cupped the animal's velvet nose with his palm in greeting, hoisted me on to its back, and together we walked out of the orchard.

The hooves of the ass, or *jinnick*, were a muffled clip-clop on the dusty road where no motor passed in an hour, but along which the children would soon be coming from school.

One day I would go to school. My father had always said so, especially since he had lately decided to settle down, so to speak, in sleepy Suffolk, and go wandering no more. No more to Tooting Bec, Highgate or Leather Lane—for gipsies, when father was a youngster, used to work the London streets and the suburbs. No more to Durham, Newcastle, Sheffield, Buxton, to Stafford, Birmingham and Norwich. Or so he said.

One day I would go to school. But what school was like he could not tell me, for he had never been. I looked at him now as we did *coor the drom* (hit the road) together; tall, he was to me, big shouldered; his *togs* were corduroy trousers with a triangle of red satin let in each leg near the hem, a shirt and scarf, bolero decorated with gilded charms and a golden sovereign. A man who filled my world, a man of mystery.

He did not remember much about where he was born. He remembered a river, and on its banks a great assembly of *tans*, or tents, where his Romany people lived in Galatz, in Romania. It was like a dream of long ago . . . the *vardos*, or caravans, the *chavis*, children barelegged and barefooted, with tousled hair.

He was told later that the river was the Danube, and he remembered that the men who worked the ships and barges on the river did not speak his language, the Romany which he and his brothers *rokkered*, or spoke, together.

The women, the *juvals*, told fortunes and made their wares for sale, sitting in circles gossiping. The men, mainly horse breeders and dealers, were often away. The children were the home-tenders, gathering driftwood for fires on which the communal food was cooked.

And it was round the fire, in darkness lit only by orange flames, that in the evening the tribe gathered to sing and dance to the wild music of the *bosh*, or fiddle. Or they would pick a quarrel and fight. (Although it is not always necessary for a Romany to have a row to start a fight. As with the Irish a fight can be begun most amicably.)

My father remembered his mother Anyeta as a beautiful dark-eyed woman; dark as a walnut and filled with life. His father whose name is from the Romany words *petul-engro*, horseshoe-maker or smith—was a Romany from Wales who had travelled afar horse-dealing, and met and married Anyeta in the wild romantic mountains of Romania.

The Welsh-Romanian gipsy boy, my father, remembered little of the towns and villages through which he journeyed in Romania, Bosnia and Hungary. The big days in his life were the fiestas and fairs where his father bartered for ponies and goats.

Then came the day his father decided to leave Anyeta's tribe and take his wife and child to Britain. The crossing was from Antwerp to Harwich, and the first stop was Barnet horse fair. Once on these kind and gentle shores my father found a race of kindly, humorous, freedom-loving and superstitious people with whom to fall in love and from whom he was rarely again parted—the English.

So, from my father I could never learn what it was like to go to school, and I could not ask the big boys who set off each weekday with satchel and sandwiches, for most of them would not speak to a gipsy.

Those first two memories: my father's—harsh perhaps, colourful, poverty-stricken and hard; my own—softer, lit by an English sun, yet in a way just as simple and spartan. . . . They are the heart of the story I want to tell—the story of my boyhood with my father, Gipsy Petulengro, in those far-off days before the motor car had completely taken over this land.

The long, straight street of Lavenham was sleepy in the afternoon heat as we walked its length that day. Stillness lay everywhere like the dust and our footsteps echoed as we passed the sun-blistered doors along the way. The dark rooms behind the windows were high-ceilinged, tall enough to take a loom, for weaving was the industry there.

On the other side of the town was our vardo, perched in true Romany tradition near a stream, in the shade of trees and not too far from a friendly farmhouse. As the gate creaked the grazing horses paused to look.

My mother on the steps of the vardo shaded her eyes as she caught sight of us and went inside to prepare a meal. The flash of her golden hair in the sun was to me like the flash of fire—warm, reassuring. But her blue eyes often held a coolness, an amusement I found disconcerting, especially if I had been wicked. I would rather face my father's roar than my mother's silence.

Now she motioned for me to wash my hands in a bowl of water while she put on the *kaba* to boil and my father tied up Tarno the donkey. Then we sat round the table in the far corner, with clean, flowered china and apostle spoons. "Now we will stir according to St John." My father's inevitable joke had become a ritual.

It must be evident by now that my father was no ordinary gipsy. Long since parted from any tribe, during his lifetime he travelled the length and breadth of England and Wales, and worked his way to America and back. Before his days of glory on the BBC programme *The World Goes By*, with Freddie Grisewood, before his days of fame as one of the first newspaper astrologers, he would deal in anything that would bring profit, from horses (about which he knew everything, although my mother was the better rider) to carpets, cutlery, jewellery made of gold wire and beads, home-made toys, tin-openers, and once an odoriferous substance which he named 'Carboniferous Ooze', for cleaning silver.

He was indeed a 'travellin' man', whose restless nature was derived from generations of true Romanies, as opposed to *poshrats* (half-bloods) and *didikais* or hedge-crawlers—all, he knew in his bones to be far lower in grade and not to be counted among the aristocrats of his line, a line that had been nomadic for two thousand years.

Our home, our vardo, was a splendid sight. On the hills of Staffordshire or Wales it had needed four horses to pull it whenever we moved on. Two were ours and two would be hired from a local farmer along with the driver.

My mother always travelled in her own little gig, sitting proud in the swaying vehicle, with her own skewbald pony trotting smartly along between the shafts.

My job was to help pull the huge brake on the vardo when it came to go down the hills, so that the horses would not be hustled into an untimely gallop by the weight.

The vardo I remember in my earliest years was lined with mahogany which Marie, my mother, polished until it looked like a red apple. She was 'house-proud', and because she was also a very good cook my father, in his more affluent days, went to the expense of having specially made for her a beautiful electro-plated cooking range.

The vardo, which he had designed and which had been built for us at Brigg, was the pride of his life. It was the first 'Pullman' on the road, but many 'showmen' later copied it in size and design.

Its total length, I suppose, was about twenty feet. And it was a good eight feet wide, too wide, in fact, to negotiate some of the more narrow *boreens* (lanes). In shape it was similar to the waggon known as the 'Burton' as opposed to the round-roofed 'Reading'. Slung under the body were lockers for storage and for packing away pots and pans and other heavy articles when we moved on.

The interior was a miracle of design in that every nook and cranny housed a cupboard or chest in which was kept china, food and clothing. It had two rooms: a bedroom with two bunks for my parents, separated by sliding doors from a living-room/kitchen where there was a padded bench for my own rest, though I much preferred to sleep outside when the weather allowed.

Panelled mirrors which were elaborately engraved and embossed graced the interior with ormolu elegance, as did the ceiling, a marvellous sight, especially for a child waking up at dawn and seeing it bathed in a pink glow. There were cherubs and scrolls worked in blue and pink, and puffy clouds, cherries and grape-vines intertwined. Even the ceiling of the Sistine Chapel had surely not been so much admired as that of our vardo.

When I was small I lived in a wonderland with these cherubs, sharing with them my childish joys and sorrows and making up a whole life for them as I lay on my bench gazing up into their world.

The vardo, so splendid, with its chocolate brown wood, the stays picked out in red and yellow and highlighted with elaborate carvings decorated in gold-leaf, fascinated everyone who came across it on its journeys.

"When's the circus coming, Mister?" yelled the village children, running alongside.

"The elephants and lions are not far behind," Xavier replied, entering into the spirit of the thing.

At one time when we were in Essex, an elderly gentleman whom the locals had nicknamed the 'mad sailor', made a suggestion. Why not cut a hole in the roof of the waggon, stick up a mast and go under sail power? My father, thinking it best to humour him, readily agreed that this was indeed a brilliant plan.

He was sorry he had acquiesced when, the next morning, with the first rays of the sun, 'sailor' appeared complete with ladder and saw to cut a hole in the roof and carry out his 'brilliant plan'. It took a great deal of effort to dissuade him, but we often spoke of his idea later when in Lincolnshire and Cambridgeshire the winds with which we had to battle were so strong that they could have done the job even without the sails.

The interior of the van, or waggon, was always very cosy, in true gipsy tradition. Besides being so beautifully planned that everything was to hand, its windows were framed in lace curtains and sheltered at night by external shutters, when the bracket oil lamps cast their mellow glow over the rooms. These lamps proved to be so hot that the stove was allowed to die down and the roof ventilators had to be opened, even on the coldest night, to let out some of the warm, used air.

I spent the long winter evenings carving wood, painting, crayonning or doing jigsaw puzzles lent by the wife of the local *givengro* (farmer) while Marie baked bread, or sewed or made pickles.

Marie was not of pure Romany stock, being descended on one side, so the rumour went, from a Norfolk farmer and horse breeder of the 1780s who, not content with gambling away his whole livelihood, had also got with child a Romany girl. She had always had a hankering after a house where she could indulge her domestic skills on a more permanent basis. In fact, some Norwegian blood, which accounted for her golden hair, flowed in her veins and this strain really came out in most of her attitudes to life, so that she acted as a brake on many of Xavier's wilder moments, and was a curbing element on my own in later years.

She had control—control of her temper and of her will and of her environment; and it was mainly due to her that I went to school, learned table manners and the like, so that, separated as I was for most of my childhood from other gipsy children, and influenced by my avenging angel of a mother, I cannot claim to have been always typical of what most people expect a Romany child to be. I might end the day as dirty as any other child, but I always went to bed clean. Everything within my mother's orbit was spotless, including me!

But enough of that, for life was certainly lived in the spirit of the travellers down the ages and my life since then has certainly borne the 'imprinting' process of those days when we did *coor the drom* together.

By all reports I had been a *boro odjus tikner*, a big, lovely baby. True to Romany tradition, I was plunged into a bath of cold water immediately after my birth, and within months my ears had been pierced ready to take the gold sleepers that by lore and by love I was to wear the rest of my life. Golden ear-rings were worn by the Romanies mainly because it was believed that they improved the vision and steadied the nerves—perhaps on the same principle as acupuncture. Besides, if a Romany who was a Christian (and thousands were) died while in a strange land then his golden ear-rings ensured a proper Christian burial, for they could be sold to pay for it.

My toys as I grew, were few and far between, but I became a friendly child, always off with anyone who would take me along, whether to pull up swedes, cut chaff or turnips, plough the fields and scatter, or to watch the good *gurnis* being milked and the *gryes* being stabled at the end of a hard working day.

My earliest toys were little acrobatic men, made by Xavier out of two bits of wood, some wire, and the button-like head of a clothes-peg. If ever I had anything from a shop like a drum or a gun, it was a thrill. I knew that my father bought these with *wongur* (money) but where he kept it I never knew. In the main, my toys were pets: Rufus, the collie dog, who slept under the vardo, *Kaulochirilo*, the tame blackbird who would feed from my hand, and Spike the *hotchi-witchi*—a young hedgehog.

When I was small, before I learned to use my fists in a fight, or to work with my wit and brawn for my bread, the living was easy. We were some time at Lavenham, then at Peldon where, at 'The Peldon Rose', 'Grandma' Pullen, my first sweetheart, took a fancy to me and insisted I sleep in one of her spare bedrooms.

Excited by the chance to sleep under a roof I granted her wish and gratified my curiosity about the *gorgio* or non-gipsy way of life. In the evening I would dance to the music of a melodion, on the long refectory table of The Peldon Rose's low-ceilinged bar. The locals threw pennies, which sometimes hurt my legs . . . but, said my father, one must suffer to be rich. My audience consisted of joskins, fishermen, coast-guards and smugglers.

My life went by in a haze of extraordinary happiness. In the mornings I was up early with my toy gun and my collie, roving the fields and lanes, gazing importantly into the trees for rooks, which were in no danger from my fake fire-arm and cawed with demoniacal derision.

The dew would be still glittering when Xavier and I gathered mushrooms at many a pink dawn. The frost was still sparkling when my mother and I went searching for red hips in the autumn glory. In successive summers I slept underneath the vardo or beneath the stars—my love-affair with 'Grandma' Pullen's house over.

In winter I was allowed to ride one of the two Suffolk Punches that pulled the plough on the local farm. Followed by screeching sea-gulls, jogging slowly to the roll of the huge, steaming horse beneath me, my breath was a white mist, my hands pink with cold as they grasped the brass-studded collar. Transfixed with joy, in my mind I owned the horse, the earth, the sky.

I could imagine no other life.

2

Romany Chal—Romany Lore

A Romany *chal* must work and before I was seven I knew what it was to have an aching back from gathering the nettles, docks and twitch-grass my father sold by the sackful to herbalists.

One day I asked him why we gathered these weeds when the farm labourers—joskins—laughed and joked about us and our foolishness. He replied: "The farmer who pays to rid his fields of these dratted weeds they call dandelions is the first to complain of rheumatics or sciatica when the frost comes.

"Off he goes to the doctor, paying anything from ten shillings for examination and prescription, then paying the chemist five more shillings to have his prescription made up. And what are the magic words scrawled on the paper he hands over the counter? *Decotium Taraxaci*—dandelion root, plain and simple, boiled in water. The finest tonic for liver, blood and rheumatic complaints.

"It's the same with nettles; look how cross he is when he sees the wicked things waving in the breeze. The sight gives him apoplexy. Yet he'll pay any fancy price for medicine for high blood pressure that contains *Urtica dioica*—the common stinging nettle by another name."

I marvelled at his wisdom and knowledge and set to with a will. He told me his mother, Anyeta, had said that nature makes the ailment and nature makes the cure. "Where there is much damp and water, there beside it grows the willow bark to cure rheumatic fevers."

He told me how the names were similar to the disease. "Chestnut leaves for the chest complaints; gravel root for stone and gravel; liver-wort for the liver; lungwort for lungs; heart's-ease for weak hearts, and even the herb called rupture-wort will ease rupture." He taught me to recognize these, to pluck them, separate and dry them for selling.

Nobody chased us or condemned us for ridding their fields and hedgerows of 'weeds'. I was astounded to find they would even pay us good money to do it. And we sold the herbs by the sackful afterwards. I soon learned the tricks of the trade; for instance, cut nettles brought us four shillings a hundred-weight more than uncut nettles, and for this little task we even had the nerve to borrow the farmer's chaff-cutter.

Nettles were part of my diet—they taste like spinach and are very good for you. People today don't know what they're missing. Take the humble dandelion. Of the flower we made wine very similar to good hock. Of the root we made a hundred remedies or we dried it for dandelion coffee; the leaves were crisp in salads. Indeed, as my father said: "The *parni-kip-lulagi*, the piddle-bed-flower, is a gift from the gods."

Apart from vegetables, *tattitatti* (baked potatoes) and herbs, my meals consisted mainly of home-baked bread and honey, goat's milk from my father's two nanny goats, fish and hare and hedgehog.

There were some animals we could not eat or have anything to do with because they were considered *mokado* (dirty, impure). These included the fox, *makadi jook* (literally, dirty dog). Other forbidden animals included the cat, any rodents and, to a degree, the dog, which meant that no dog was allowed in the vardo, but had to sleep underneath.

The handling of a dog was all right, but it was never

allowed to lick your face, and if it ate from a bowl, that bowl could not be washed up with the other implements used for the family meal. However, many Romany families had good and faithful guard dogs, although these were never spoilt and petted. My father taught me when I was still very young how to keep a dog as a friend for life. He would place a piece of bread under his armpit to become impregnated in sweat and then hand it to the dog to eat. It never failed.

The carrion-crow was also considered impure, but never the horse, the donkey, goats or a cow, or any song birds. These were not for eating—most of them were family friends, in fact.

Anyeta told me that in olden days no Romany ate animal flesh unless he could find nothing else, and then he was supposed to kill only animals with bristles such as the wild boar or the domestic *grunter* or a *hotchi-witchi* (hedgehog).

I have only tasted hedgehog once, and I can say that the flesh was incredibly delicious, while my father insisted that hedgehog fat made the best ointment for healing wounds in the world.

Yet we would rarely wish to kill a little hedgehog, being as they are, immune to any plant or animal poisons, and able to eat every sort of farm and field pest. I used to have a pet one called Spike who lived to a ripe old age, and I loved to watch him backing into his lair, so that his delicate nose should not be damaged as he entered. His death, from the wheels of a motor car, was a source of immense sorrow and grief to me.

A Romany must catch his own *matchi* (fish) to eat. No trip to the fishmonger in our day. We ate eels from streams, and on a day's outing to the Suffolk and Essex coast my father and I would gather cockles and mussels, winkles and whelks. The streams gave up trout, which we tickled, or baited with oils of rhodium, juniper and cedar-wood all sprinkled on a handful of moss in which worms were then placed for twelve hours. No trout could resist it.

Tickling was a fine art which I learned early in childhood. I would lie down close to the water, slowly place my arm in the stream and gently stroke a drowsy trout, swiftly flip the fish on to the ground beside me. The number of times I fell in before I perfected my tickling does not bear thinking of—it was how I learned to swim.

As I grew older I spent many a long hour by quiet streams where I had no business, fishing for trout or roach or pike. I learned to listen for the footfall of the *weshengro* (gamekeeper) like an Indian. For pike we dropped a three-angled hook weighted with a small leaden ball the size of a marble, on thick line, about a foot away from the lurking fish which likes to laze in muddy shallows. We gave a quick twist of the line and hooked him in the gills before waiting for him to bite.

Besides learning to tickle trout, I, like every true Romany boy, was taught to speak my own language, play the fiddle and understand that I must never hit a *gorgio* with a stick (hit him with your fists!). I was taught to barter, to sell, how to shout my wares at a market stall or charm a housewife at the door.

My father taught me how to recognize types of people from their house or garden, for the Romany pedlar must know what to expect when the door opens.

"Lion," he said, "look at the windows first. If the curtains are generous in material and the blinds are rolled up crooked, expect an untidy, kind-hearted woman. When the curtains are draped in an exact loop and the blinds pulled up tightly, you'll find a calculating tyrant. Where the curtains are skimped you'll find a mean, mistrustful female. And nine times out of ten the woman with a badly polished door knocker opens her door and shouts: 'We don't want any tramps in *this* house.'

"An old maid's garden has plants stuck in anywhere; people give her cuttings and she puts them in any vacant space. Nor is anything ever thinned out. The garden is a riot of colour in the summer—and you'll always find her good for a talk and a sale."

He continued: "Then there is the calculating garden, prim, austere, with the roses trained nicely. This is a lady who needs much persuasion and has to be in a very good temper to listen or buy. Happy-go-lucky people like rock-gardens—little or no work to do, no digging; where there is a rock-garden there is nearly always a kind soul. And always keep an eye open for the child's corner where he grows what he fancies— where there are children you will not get a stern rebuff."

These early lessons in psychology, which my father gave me, have always been of great help and I have learned to sum up a person or a situation in an instant. Yet it was Anyeta, chief of the tribe, and not my father, who was responsible for much of my education in those early years. Her word was law.

She did not live with us but with my father's cousin and his tribe, the Lovells, who travelled mainly in Cambridgeshire and the central counties of England, although sometimes they would wander to Wales—always a favourite place of Anyeta's, for it was from those mountains and valleys that her late husband had come to Romania to woo her many a long year ago.

As my *puridaia* (grandmother) I respected her, but loved her, too, and would sit at her feet to listen to her wisdom for hours on end.

"Now, *chav, av akai, ki mandi* (now, my child, come here to me) and I shall *rokker ki tooti* (talk to you) and you will listen and it will be better than any *lil* (book), for I will *pen* the Romany lore so you will not grow up a *dindilo* (idiot) and it is in this way that you will always be *bakalo* (lucky)." And Anyeta would puff on her pipe, her skin brown like a nut, her face crazed with lines from wind and weather, but her dark eyes a-twinkle with wisdom and humour.

"Your life is to work. Work is honour and laziness is of the *beng* (the devil). You may steal every seven years, but no more; it is allowed to the Romanies; and that is all. But, *dordi, dordi*, we have suffered much from the *posh-rats, mumpers, pikies* and *didikais* who steal all the time and give us a *narked nav* (bad name) with their *mumpli* ways.

"You must not question what your elders *pooker* (tell you) for they know wisdom and you *nanti* (don't). You must not question them or argue with them, and you must always do the work that you are told to do. If you are sent to collect water, you do it. If you are put to carving *faida* (pegs), you do it; if you are told to groom the *gryes* you will set to, and it is in this way you will learn what it is to be a Rom.

"You will, when you are older, learn to *kor* (fight) like a true Rom with your fists and *nanti* with a *kosh* (never with a stick). One day when you are a Rom you will *rommer* (marry); choose a Romany *raklo* for she will be a *kooshti monisha* (good wife). She will not meddle with your business for she is there to cook and clean and tend to the waggon, *bikining* (selling) from door to door and *dukkerin* (hand-reading). And if she is not a *kooshti monisha* you may beat her, but she may hit you, too, if she is a lively *joovi*. And if you are a good Rom you will never be *lullered by the gavvers* (arrested by the police), or come before the *blistering moosh* (magistrate).

"And you will have *chavis*, and you will *pooker* them the Romany lore that I *rokker* now to you."

Anyeta was short and to the point in her tutoring, for the harsh days of gipsy tribal lore were long over, and it was no longer necessary for the many ritual rules to be obeyed, or for a woman to give all her earnings to her husband or the head of the tribe. There is much talk of Romanies being 'free', but until only seventy years ago they were rigidly hemmed about by traditions and laws and an ordinary Romany man, part of the tribe, would work all day for his tribal chief and have little money for himself at the end of it. A strict code ensured that he kept only a small part for himself, just like today's income tax system where a large proportion of one's earnings are taken away for the supposed good of the whole nation. His work must be perfect and finished on time. If he was discovered to be dishonest he could be punished or even killed by the tribe's chief.

A woman's lot was harsh indeed, and when Anyeta was young she had known what it was like to have a beating. Unfaithfulness was out of the question, for if he found out her husband could have had her buried alive by his *prals* (brothers).

Her people had strict morals. There was never a divorce in the family, nor a girl expecting an illegitimate child, nor a Rom running off with someone else's wife. In Anyeta's youth she could not speak to another man, especially a *gorgio* man, without her husband's permission; nor could she be served in a shop by a man.

Xavier was more modern in his outlook, but I remember well the occasions on which his inbred Romany jealousy came to the fore. Marie was, in her youth, a beauty. One day in a village where they had newly arrived, she and my father went to buy some meat from the butcher's shop. There were two men inside the shop, so Marie waited outside, as usual, while Xavier, a natural gourmet and connoisseur, went in to do the shopping.

The butcher, who had not seen them arrive together, while serving Xavier suddenly became aware of the angel standing outside his window.

"Well," he announced to my father with a wink. "I wouldn't mind sleeping with *her*."

"Well," said my father in reply, "I do. Take *this*," and his huge fist flashed in a straight right to the jaw. As the butcher disappeared suddenly below counter level Xavier strode out of the shop never to return.

Marie, true to Romany tradition, never wore a low-necked blouse, nor had a button undone, nor dealt at the door with a man, always asking for the lady of the house, nor did she ever take off her button-boots in front of anyone, man or woman.

A woman was never the equal of her man and was banned from the Tribal Council until she had passed the age of child-bearing. But after that, if she showed herself to be rich in wisdom, she could become chief of the tribe, as had Anyeta on her husband's death. Before that time *all* her earnings and those of her children while young, had to be yielded to the common purse.

Anyeta had never quite forgiven Xavier, her son, for separating from the tribe, but was proud of his success in the sphere of a salesman, and would listen to his tales of London and 'the Ditch' (Houndsditch where he traded for most of his wares) for hours.

"Ah," she would tell me with a wink, "he is a *wafodi Rom* (a bad one), that one, but he do make good *bunce* (profit). Now scarper, *Tarno Roy*, (now run away little Prince) for you must soon *kip*." And a far-away look would come into her eyes as she puffed on her pipe and watched the evening star appear in the still blue sky.

There were many more things I learned of Romany life as I grew up; I would always ask Anyeta "Why? Why?" To receive her answer: "Because it is the Romany lore."

Each member of our family had his or her own plate, cup, fork, knife and spoon. No husband or wife ever drank out of the same cup, even though it was considered quite clean to drink from a stream after a horse—though never after a dog. If a fly or bluebottle was found on food or a plate, the food had to be thrown away at once. In our vardo there were spare sets of dishes for entertaining *gorgio* visitors. Other Romanies brought their own dishes.

The observance of domestic rules was strict and no Romany woman would dream of breaking them any more than she would think of passing in front of her husband where he was sitting, always behind him. At night time she never went to bed before her husband, and always allowed him to sleep nearest the wall so that she could rise before him without disturbing him.

In a Romany family there is one very strict rule about the serving of food. The eldest is always served first. It is a sin for a child to be greedy, and he must always wait for his serving last without showing signs of impatience.

But we Romany *chals* never resented this treatment of the old. We revered wrinkles, loved the old for their wisdom and cherished them for their understanding of life.

And so I grew up learning Romany lore at Anyeta's knee, but my formal education began at eight when my parents decided to send me to school. I must have been through more village schools than any other child of my generation. At each new school I ran the gauntlet of derision when my pierced ears and gold sleepers were noticed. The fights this started, I won.

"Gipsy, gippo. No shoes, no shoes!" The cries which followed me in the playground earned their instigators a black eye or bloody nose apiece.

But the rough, tough ten-year-old gipsy found that his heart was soft, for he fell in love with a *gorgio* girl in the next class. From our classroom we boys could see the girls through a glass divide. My infatuation was so intense that unfortunately my master, Mr Pratt, noticed my pre-occupation with the activities next door. "If I find you looking that way again, you can go and sit with the girls."

He was as good as his word and within days I found myself, by arrangement with the mistress, Miss Wackett, joining the girls for reading, writing, 'rithmetic and sewing. Thus was my passion for Mary-Anne and her auburn curls doused. The hilarity of the boys next door, their grinning faces, noses flattened by the glass partition, was the cause of my beetroot face while I clumsily stitched away at lazy-daisy.

3

Rufus

My father had found him by the roadside. He was obviously in bad shape, a saddened, abandoned male puppy with pain and suspicion in his eyes, and he snarled when he was touched, more in pain than anger perhaps.

Xavier patted his head. "Good boy, good boy, Rufus." He seemed to have struck lucky. The puppy responded by licking his hand. He felt the place where the ribs stood out, testifying to hunger. The pup's paws were bleeding from some long journey, and as he struggled to his feet Xavier could see that the hip was injured.

He was a lovely animal, long in the leg, with long silky hair—black, white and slate blue. His ears were pointed and continually twitching back and forth to catch every sound.

After some persuasion Xavier got him into his arms and took him along to the village vet, who agreed to keep him for a week or two and see to the injured hip; in the meantime he told the police of the existence of a stray dog. He had no collar, so no one could trace his previous owners, only guess that here was an abandoned gipsy lurcher—not a crime that true Romanies ever perpetrated, but even in those days the gipsy colony was made up of tinkers and *didikais* and all manner of flotsam, and Xavier supposed that, moving on, they decided to abandon the injured pet rather than pay the vet's fees. Of course, when no one had claimed the pup after two weeks, Xavier couldn't resist him, and eventually Rufus became mine.

I remember that day well. My father had not told me of his find, knowing that once my curiosity was roused I'd want to see the dog, and should he have to be put down then the disappointment would be too much for me. When Rufus recovered and the vet offered him to Xavier, he gladly took charge of the puppy and brought him home secretly one night to the vardo, long after I was asleep.

The puppy slept quietly that night, showing no antagonism to his new owners, nor any dislike of his new house on wheels. He had the collie's usual beautiful fierce awareness of life and would prove to be a good watch-dog, for his nose twitched like a rabbit's and his ears went up every time there was a noise. And he'd give a low growl deep in his throat before returning to a light sleep from which, it appeared, the slightest sound could wake him.

I slumbered on, unaware of our new companion, or the role that he would play in my life. The next morning, I sat on the window-seat waiting for my bread and milk breakfast (horrible, soppy thought—I can't tell you why I liked such fare).

"Open the lid of the seat," Xavier commanded, grinning. "Come on, Lion, stir yourself *chal*." Wondering, I jumped down from my perch and opened what might as well have been Pandora's box, for all the reverence I gave it. What could be inside? A new toy? A new tool for working on some novel and unwelcome scheme of my father's to make money? I was three years old and already knew his habits and his predelictions well. I could not really believe that the chest could contain anything to delight me.

The puppy looked up warily from the depths, its eyes gleaming with a kind of wolfish fear. I shrieked with joy and grabbed him, only to be bitten for my good nature. There was blood, a scream from Marie, a roar from Xavier and a sob of pain from me. In the pandemonium the puppy escaped

30

and crouched under the table, as if at bay against the enemy. Then I felt the tentative kiss of friendship as a cold, wet muzzle was thrust into my hand. He was sorry. It was all a mistake.

He was immediately forgiven, and so we began our ten years of friendship. Xavier gave me the wisdom of the Romanies concerning dogs, anxious that I should be the master in this alliance.

"Listen Lion, first give him some bread which you have chewed in your own mouth. The taste and scent of the saliva will be an imprinting process the dog will never forget. Then put a piece of bread under your armpit for a while to absorb some sweat—he'll always know who is his master when he has tasted that, boy.

"Give him plenty of discipline right from the start. Don't beat him, but when you give him a command make it quite clear that you expect to be obeyed without question. A tap on the nose is far more effective than a beating.

"Always be to time, where possible, in your routine, Lion. Serve his meal at the same time each day and never fail him; that way he will trust you and you may trust him.

"But most important of all in a dog's training is praise. If you are pleased, show it. Pat him and scratch his ears, get him to recognize the phrase 'good dog'. It is all he has in the way of reward—your approval, your affection, and he'll respond to that every time."

So spake Xavier.

The dog was a revelation to me. From that moment we were hardly ever apart, except on the sad occasions when I had to attend school. Even then he would sometimes make up his mind to attend, too. He had a way of inspecting any new school I went to, just to see if he approved of the establishment within whose walls I was incarcerated for so many hours each day.

I remember the sound of his feet pattering up and down the

31

lines of children when we were at prayer in assembly, until he found me. Then, satisfied that I was well and truly alive, although strangely incommunicado, he'd sit patiently beside me until prayers were over.

Different teachers took this strange phenomenon in different ways, according to their personalities.

"Whose dog is that?"

"Mine, sir."

"And what is he doing here?"

"Please, sir, he just followed me."

"Well, get him out of here."

That was usually the reaction of the men. The women were softer in their approach, and some made a pet of him. At Sudbury in Suffolk he was almost the school mascot.

He enjoyed these excursions into the classroom enormously, but learnt nothing, content to snooze all though reading and writing, but shocked out of his somnolence by the recital of 'tables' during arithmetic.

True to Romany tradition, Rufus slept outside the vardo, and once he was fully grown, was rarely allowed across the threshold. His favourite place during our travels was on the doorstep, seated importantly between my father and myself, leaning his furry side against mine in a passion of trust, watching the road and barking impertinently at innocent passers-by.

The dog, according to Romany lore, is *mokado*—dirty. He is not counted such a friend as the horse. But Rufus, with his charm, broke down most of my father's ingrained resistance to such a relationship with a dog as actual friendship. He would even talk to him as an equal, ask his advice, and throw sticks for him to retrieve.

No true Romany ever plays with a dog—it's beneath his dignity!

Rufus was two years old when we nearly lost him. I was young enough to count the whole thing a great tragedy and

My father, Gipsy Petulengro, gazing into his crystal ball!

'The Peldon Rose' in Peldon where 'Grandma' Pullen presided and I danced across the tables

had I the strength and the weapons there would have been blood on my hands.

For Rufus got mixed up in a sheep-worrying dispute when we were in the Welsh border country called the Marches, and very narrowly escaped death by the gun.

We had been pitched for several days in a sheltered valley by a stream, happy to be once again on my grandfather's terrain, his homeland, and doing a brisk trade with the farmers' wives in all manner of hardware that Xavier had bought up and transported from the nearest industrial towns of the Midlands.

Come evening, as the pale autumn sun set and the harvest moon rose above the rounded mountains, giving the country-side that mysterious bloom of a purple grape set against silver mercury, a cross and red-faced sheep farmer invaded our peaceful encampment with loud and indignant threats. He carried a shotgun across his arm, its barrel broken where it should be, for safety; but you could see by his eyes that it would only take a second to straighten it and aim with deadly intent.

"Hey gippo. What are you doing, letting that b—— dog of yours run free on them hills? He's worrying the sheep and that's a crime in these parts. If I see him again he'll be a gonner!"

He tapped his trusty two-bore. My father responded, springing to his feet and squaring up to the man, who shrank back a little when he realized the discrepancy in height and breadth of shoulder, about three inches in each case.

"You shut your mouth, *wafodi gorgio*. No dog of mine would do such a thing. You can be quite sure of that." Xavier clenched his huge fists, and my five-year-old mind grew hazy with the excitement of anticipating the fight. I had seen him in battle only once, and seeing he was upon that occasion the victor, I wished to see him fight again, although I was afraid of the gun.

33

The farmer retreated to the place from which he had sprung—a gap in the hedgerow, muttering threats, though with less vehemence or conviction.

All this time Rufus had watched silently, lying with head between his paws. It struck me as strange that he had not warned us of the farmer's approach with his usual growl, then rising to his feet and pointing his body in the direction of the intruder. He had not stirred throughout the whole interview. It was as if he knew the discussion was about him and that his life was in danger. He had taken to straying from the vardo for several hours at a time during our stay in this lovely part of the borderlands, but we had thought he was merely chasing rabbits.

"Better keep him chained up in future," said Xavier to me brusquely. But he knew the responsibility was really his own; at five I was too young to be in constant control of a dog, however faithful the animal.

My mother seemed reluctant to leave our lovely spot, despite the fact that an Indian summer turned to a brilliant autumn, and soon the frosty mornings meant a continuous watch on the fire. Xavier was impatient to be off, but she seemed in love with the place, and so we stayed on, with Xavier leaving us from time to time to get more goods from Birmingham, selling them on his journeys to and from town, and seeing us only once or twice in a fortnight.

It was an idyllic time for both me and my mother. We gathered the sweet autumnal fruits, kept our toes warm by the vardo stove at night, roamed the slopes in search of mushrooms during the day, bought butter and milk from the nearest dairy farm, all of five miles away, and talked to everyone along the way.

The night of Xavier's return was a dark and stormy one. Rain fell in great waving curtains from the leaden skies, and the hills loomed in menacing fashion around us, sentinels, brooding, dark and locked in mystery. Next morning we heard two shots. Rufus had been missing all night, but this had become almost routine during Xavier's absence and there was nothing to be done in such a dreadful storm.

The dawn broke, pink and calm after the turbulence. A robin trilled in the hedge, the only brave bird to sing its song in winter. Crows were circling above as Rufus limped into our little encampment, bedraggled, wet from his shiny nose to his no-longer feathery tail. It was obvious by the way the dog was behaving that he wanted me to go with him. He ran towards me then ran away again towards the base of the hills, then returned. He would take no food, but drank from the stream, and then, giving a last look of appeal in my direction, trotted off to the East.

My parents, breakfasting, had not known of his return. I decided to follow him by myself.

I set off across the fields by the stream towards the biggest hill and following the dog I began to climb. It was a feat of mountaineering for a five-year-old boy to cope with wiry grass, then gravel and loose scree, then rocks. The sun rose higher in the sky as I climbed, Rufus's flash of white tail in front all the while. We were over the shoulder now, out of sight of my parents or any civilization. Sheep fled before us on the hillside, and I saw that Rufus took no notice of them at all. So much for the farmer's suspicions.

We had come to a cave and inside, in a nest made from some sacks, long forgotten by other shelterers, was a squirming bundle of blind puppies. Their squeaking had a note of distress, and I could figure out why. It seemed that Rufus was the father of these shaggy and still damp little beauties, but where was their mother? The young puppies were in great need of her milk.

I sat down to play with the puppies, cuddling and stroking them while they anxiously sucked my fingers, and tried to work out what had happened. Rufus stood proudly but anxiously by, giving the moving mass a nudge every now and again. And so we sat all morning, keeping the pups warm, waiting for help. I somehow knew that if I left them they would die of exposure, for Rufus lacked the maternal instinct to cover them.

My parents' cries could be heard at midday as they came up the last steep slope through dead bracken. I ran to meet them and was rewarded with a clip on the ear from a furious Xavier. Marie cradled my head and cried with relief. A farm labourer had seen Rufus and me disappearing over the brow of the hill two hours previously and had reported the matter to them.

Rufus came now to meet them wagging his tail, for here was help at last.

"That *wafodi* dog!" my father roared. "I thought he was dead. That cursed farmer told me he killed him last night, boy, chasing sheep, but it was so black he couldn't trace the carcass. Yet here he is, large as life."

Rufus and I showed them the pups. My mother was immediately enchanted. She took off her shawl and, placing them inside, insisted on starting back at once.

"They'll die if we don't get some milk into them quickly, Xavier. Come!"

But there was one more thing Rufus wanted us to see. My father followed him while I went with my mother. On the other shoulder of the hill lay the explanation of the farmer's tale. A huge and lovely white bitch lay dead, a bullet through her heart. Rufus mourned her, sitting at her side as the sun sank until my father buried her on the mountainside while the 'wait-until-dark' crows cawed disappointedly.

"Get off, you buggers," shouted my father with satisfaction, as he and Rufus made for home.

We often talked about what had really happened that night. No one ever came forward to say the bitch was his or hers, no villager ever remembered seeing the animal around at all. No sheep were found to be missing or killed, but there was evidence that they had been worried recently, and in the half-light it had seemed to be Rufus to the farmer. Yet how could a heavily pregnant bitch worry sheep?

We brought up the puppies and gave them away on travels to people who would give them good homes. I was sorry to see them go, but mother said we could not keep them. Rufus, the widower, once his progeny were safely in our hands, lost interest!

"Well, old fellow," said Xavier when at last we were back in Suffolk and the last puppy had gone. "That was an adventure, for sure. And we'll never know the truth of it."

Rufus looked wise and said nothing.

4

Jack of all Trades

During our travels my father changed occupations with startling frequency. He was nothing if not opportunist. I remember the day he parted with a nanny-goat to a school-boy—thus cutting our milk production by half—in exchange for a camera, a tripod, a hood, some plates and set himself up as village photographer.

Now we were down to one nanny-goat and a billy-goat. Now Billy was a problem, for he had a temper. His pet aversion was a stick and to wave one in front of him was to invite a certain fate and some very impressive bruises.

One Sunday my father told me not to stand around idle (the worst sin for a Romany boy) but to take the goats to the stream for a drink. There we were peacefully grazing—I dreamily chewing a hazel twig while they made short work of a whole branch—when down the lane came the Sudbury branch of the Salvation Army. As soon as I saw the drummer I knew there was trouble in store.

Billy saw him too, doing all the twirls and twiddles and fancy stuff that to him must have looked like rude provocation indeed. Down went his head before I could grasp him and off he went like a bullet from a gun.

That drum was never before banged so hard as when it was banged by Billy. I made a dive for him but he eluded me and

Jack of all Trades

raced round to the other side of the petrified drummer with
the same result. That little episode cost me months of hard
saving.

But, to return to father's venture as a photographer. It was
with surprised indignation that my mother accosted a sign-
painter who arrived at our vardo in my father's absence.
"What are you doing?"

"Why ma'am, I be aggona paint that sign, like that
gennelman want . . ." My mother knew better than to contra-
dict an order from my father but dared not ask what the sign
was to be.

After two hours he had finished, and I read for my mother
in an awed voice the magic legend: 'The Anglo-American
Photographic Company'. Evidently my father meant big
business. And it was a fair success. Small towns and villages in
those days having no photographers, there was quite a bit of
custom.

Village schools needed a photographer for class leavers.
The local butcher desired a photograph of himself and his
staff outside the shop, with 'Purveyor of First Class Meat'
written up above the dangling carcasses. Publicans bought
pictures of their pubs. Farmers and their wives wanted
portraits, solo, together, two generations, three. And there
were weddings, of course, as well as funeral parties.

As soon as he reached a new village it was my father's habit
to make friends with the *plastramengro* (peace-maker) or policeman, the parson and the publican. The *mulled-mooshengro*
(dead man maker) or doctor, and the *drabengro* (poison-
maker) or chemist, he had no use for.

Advertising by word of mouth is always best, and soon
word got about that the *mug-fakir* (photographer) had arrived.
Well scrubbed, high-collared farm-hands would be lent a
bowler hat and gold watch-chain which my father reserved
for the occasion to add a bit of style. He also took to carrying
round a potted palm for background atmosphere.

39

At night my parents sometimes worked into the small hours developing and printing. The Anglo-American Photographic Company succeeded through sheer cheek and hard work, which was ever my father's magic mixture.

Typically, within a year he had forgotten the *mug-fakir* role and set up as The Miller Manufacturing Company in an empty storeroom near Colchester, where he made gipsy jewellery with gold wire and beads. When I asked him why we were now the Millers he explained that a local printer had sold him at a reduced price headed paper and invoices of a company now dead—but not forgotten, for its soul went marching on under my father's eccentric management.

These erstwhile commercial adventures signalled my father's metamorphosis from a country Romany, who once travelled with the tribe and dealt only in country matters, to the travelling salesman and, later, showman, who became a nationwide figure of fame.

His commercial sallies were often profitable and amusing, for he was cute, had a sharp and a persuasive tongue and an uproarious sense of fun. Xavier was not a rogue or a cheat, he always worked hard and legitimately for his living, but, as many people discovered, he was a roguish personality.

As a child I never knew whether he was being serious or not. Many a time I would take some information delivered with a dead-pan expression to be gospel, only to be told later by Marie that it was lies. Poetic licence is, perhaps, the correct euphemism. I certainly loved my father, and although I could not always trust what he said, I could as a child always trust his love.

He was warm, protective, informative, and, as the Americans say, fun-loving. He talked to me as an equal—even as a tiny child—about life and about people. He was a magnificent bear of a man who believed in expressing his love with great bear hugs or by boxing or cuffing my ears, lightly throwing me in the air and catching me, and until I was quite grown up, was not averse to the warm-hearted kiss of greeting on the cheek.

Much of his humour was straight music hall. For instance, whenever he was teaching me how to sell at a stall in Colchester market he would verse me in some sparkling repartee. His wares varied from day to day but I remember when, one morning, they consisted of a toothpaste which was said to be magical in its effect. Though he never used anything but coarse salt or powdered charcoal for cleaning his own teeth, he was profuse in his praise of this pink confection that he sold for a penny a pot. However, transfixed though they might be by his line of patter, nobody among his audience seemed to be buying.

Now, I have always had a marvellous set of *dands* (to this day I have never sat in a dentist's chair). Taking advantage of this, my father grasped me one day by the shoulder as I stood in the front rank of onlookers, and asked me to open my mouth for everyone's inspection.

"One of my best customers, ladies and gentlemen. He started using my product a year ago. Look at the result." He gave my head a pat.

"Never seen me in your life before have you, little boy?"

"No, Father," came the reply, loud and clear. The onlookers doubled up; from that moment the sales boomed. As Sir Winston Churchill once said when we met at the Woodford fête and began to discuss speechifying (he had congratulated me on my fairground spiel): "If you find their attention is wandering, do as I do, put in a bloody joke." It was good advice, but I'd heard it before; it was my father's technique.

Xavier's trips to Houndsditch were becoming increasingly frequent, for he could sell all sorts of things at a profit. And, after all, he was doing country communities a service, because many manufactured goods were not well distributed, indeed, they were hardly distributed at all and there were in those days no mail order catalogues, nor trendy supermarkets in every provincial town, merely the rather dignified emporium known as the 'Draper's', whose goods were often of a limited nature.

Xavier sold clocks, hairbrushes, combs, handmirrors, vases, ornaments, cutlery, costume jewellery. If he wasn't selling from a market, he'd be holding auctions in a rented shop. When he tired of that he turned to something else.

Some years later he invented a rug-knitter which he had made up in Birmingham. Because it was a speedy rug-maker he called it the 'Maxim Rug-Knitter' after the gun of the same name. On his billheads ran the legend: "makes a rug in an hour". Naturally it didn't specify what size of rug.

Later, at a time when fashionable girls had a lot of pleats on their dresses, he invented a pleating machine. It consisted as far as I can remember, of a set of strips of metal, ordered to the length you required. You'd take your skirt and press the pleats with a hot iron and a cloth over the top and, as you pressed, you'd pull the metal out and there'd be lovely box pleats, precise in their measurement.

Another invention was a tin-opener, 'The Centrifugal', which he demonstrated beautifully to the women who gathered round open-mouthed to see him using it with the strength of his little finger. It sold in hundreds, but, of course, not one woman had stopped to think about the fact that he was a very strong man, and what he could do was probably impossible for them. It was quite a difficult opener for a woman to use unless she was built like a prize bullfighter.

He bought beads and rolled-gold wire and made necklaces of coloured beads joined by little 's' shapes of wire, which looked considerably neater than beads all strung together on thread. The female customers loved them. I didn't, however, as it was my job to thread the beads in the evening by the light of our oil lamps, and it tried my eyes.

He also made a ring, which was supposed to be lucky, out of gold wire. The wire was wound round and round a piece of shaped and graded wood, at the thickness which matched the customer's finger. Then the ends of the wire were cut and the strands of gold wire bashed out flat to form a perfect ring. This was set with a coloured stone which he would match to the customer's Zodiac sign. "Are you a Taurean, madam? Ah, I thought so. Blue is your colour, the colour of Venus. Your ring gem must be blue." They always believed him and went away happy. Looking back I always think he dealt in happiness rather than the specific wares of the moment. He had a lot of warmth and joy to give in those days.

His inventiveness was amazing, and I remember well my trips to the printer, Mr Nunn.

"What's your father up to this time?" he'd ask, squinting through rimless *pince-nez* at the latest order, written by me to Xavier's dictation, complete with drawing of how to set out the print.

One of the labels Nunn printed in colour was for 'Carboniferous Ooze', the silver cleaner, complete with a picture of a Victorian parlourmaid. Another was for a substance named 'Parla', which was a magic stain-remover, mixed in a galvanized bath from some secret recipe and sold in bottles which I hawked from door to door. It was, in fact, a very good stain-remover, and worked particularly well as a whitener of butchers' chopping boards, which was the market we eventually tamed, forsaking the housewife and her smaller commissions for 'trade'.

His 'Sun Brite' sold at 2d a packet. This was salt with something else mysteriously mixed in. Just a pinch would clean the wick of an oil lamp, and the flame would burn brighter. On the packet Mr Nunn went to town with a realistic picture of the rising sun.

Many years later, when I was quite fifteen, he took the jewellery business to Jersey, selling from a counter in one of the big shops of St Helier. My main memory of our stay there was that apart from having my digs paid for, I was given no more for my own use than seven shillings a week, which did not encompass the type of entertainment demanded by my Jersy lily of a girl friend. Unaccustomed as I was to the demands of young ladies, especially beautiful *gorgio* ones, I had to forgo the more expensive nightspots. In any case, Xavier kept a firm hand on me: "I don't mind you going to Billy's Lido," he'd say, (where the drinks were soft and the music loud), "but the Striped Monkey is forbidden." I never discovered why.

These commercial ventures of my father were often embarrassing to me for I seemed to lack in those days his rumbustious flamboyance. For instance, he took to wearing an enormous black sombrero-type of headgear when he went out, which allied to his great hoops of golden ear-rings and his moustache, worried me for some reason.

"Why do you wear that hat?" I asked him once when I was still quite young. "Everyone is looking at you."

"You silly *dindilo*," he answered, "I wear it so that they *do* look at me, of course." If he had lived decades later he would have explained to me that it was part of his 'lifestyle'. As it was I had to be content with this simple explanation and the humiliation of being called fool.

When helping him in Colchester market I sometimes felt as if I could hide away under the trestle table which was his stall when I spotted my school classmates grinning in the crowd. But it had to be borne. I had been sent to school at my mother's wish to learn some manners and the ways of a gentleman, and at my father's wish to get some sense knocked into my head along with my letters. Yet I remained apart, the Romany *chal*.

Later I made one or two attempts at respectable *gorgio* careers—mainly, I suspect, because I preferred *gorgio* girls (indeed I didn't meet many Romany ones as I grew older) and wished to become part of their way of life. I wanted to live the kind of life she would demand should I marry one.

Once I took a job in a factory. Clocking in amazed me. When the gates clanged shut behind me I felt like a caged animal; as a result I got through my job as store-keeper in double quick time thinking that when the work was done I could leave, but was horrified to learn that I must stay until the hooter went. That job, needless to say, did not last long.

When I was fifteen my father dressed me in pin-stripe trousers and a black jacket and sent me to London to Pontings bargain basement to sell his 'Neversag' curtain rods.

Today these expanding rods are in every home, keeping the net curtains in place, but in those days they were a fairly new idea. For demonstration purposes I had two wooden window frames; on one was an old bit of string with saggy curtains, on the other the wonderful 'Neversag' supporting pristine white nets.

"Don't let your neighbours see your curtains looking like this, ladies," pointing to the first window. "No, this is the way," and with a flourish I'd hook my finger round the 'Neversag' and pull it, then let it *bang* back into place. I liked that!

Mr Thomas, the Welshman who was head of Pontings, walked through the store every morning in dress coat and top hat, starting at 9.30 a.m. in the bargain basement and proceeding to the uppermost reaches of this world-famous emporium. He nodded in a friendly way to me, for he knew my father.

I did fairly well, working at selling the 'Neversag' at tuppence a yard, not shy of the customers, but terrified of the giggling sales girls who made me blush.

One day I sold not a thing; not a yard, not a foot, not an inch of 'Neversag' had changed hands by 2.30 p.m. I was just ruminating on what my father would say when he came to see me and collect his share of the takings (he had placed me in digs at Hammersmith under the eye of a kindly landlady), when a strange and gorgeous sight met my eyes.

45

An Indian prince in full regalia turban, jewels, rings, silk robes approached, followed by an entourage of about twelve people. The Prince eyed the two windows, fingered the 'Neversag', looked at me and said: "I will take as much as you have." Then, motioning to one of his followers to pay me, strode on. The aide told me that the Prince thought the 'Neversag' ideal for mosquito nets.

That was a fitting climax to my life as a bargain basement salesman. I am pleased to say I have never been in one since. The lack of air made me feel ill. Although I complained to my father once or twice his only reply was the one he had given me ten years earlier when the pennies of the yokels and farmers hit my legs in the Peldon Rose Inn as I danced on the table. "You must suffer to be rich." My share had been 2s 6d a week.

5

The Wisdom of Anyeta

Anyeta was known as the 'medicine woman' of her tribe. She knew the old Romany remedies from many countries and was thought to be especially wise in her understanding of *pattriensis* (herbs) and their curative powers.

Her lectures on this subject were lengthy, punctuated by pauses as she puffed on her clay pipe and gazed into the dying embers of the fire. However long the pause, even Xavier dared not interrupt for fear of angering her.

Hear her on broom flowers from the heathland: "Broom flowers are a cure for yaller jaundice, and mixed with bramble leaves it be the best medicine for all sorts of kidney troubles."

And on the subject of comfrey: "For all lung and chest troubles there is no better remedy than such an *odjus* (beautiful) little herb of the *drom* (wayside) that you will find lying on the ground by many a ditch or bank of a stream. When I was a *tarno joovi* (young woman) I did know a *moosh* who was old indeed who had a young grandchild and she was *nafli* (ill) of the consumption. Her he cured by making her to suck the stems of comfrey."

One of Anyeta's favourite remedies for a cough was ever to administer comfrey *meski* (tea) which she made in later years, when I knew her, from the dried herb bought from the herbalist, and stewed in water. When this was cold it was taken in quantities equivalent to a wineglassful with some

47

honey and lemon night and morning. The cough soon disappeared.

Another good herb for the cough was coltsfoot, which is very efficacious in dealing with asthma, bronchitis, and chest troubles. Some country folk know it as coughwort, and others as horse hoof. Anyeta's remedy was a handful of the leaves in a quart of water simmered until reduced to a pint, strained and poured over sliced lemon then sweetened with honey, allowed to cool, and taken by the wineglassful night and morning.

If anyone were to ask Anyeta about rheumatism she was loud in her praise of potatoes. Village women who came to her for advice were told this: "Take a raw potato, missus, and wash it well and sew it in a little bag and wear it near yourself, in a pocket or under a skirt. Carry it always, that is of great importance. In time it will pucker and grow dry, but it does not matter, for while you carry it your rheumatism will grow less and less. The potato has a powerful magic which sends a shock through the body. Then, too, you must eat some good celery."

If celery was not available, then celery seed boiled in milk and water and left to cool after straining should be drunk three times a day. This was Anyeta's way of dealing with the scourge of rheumatism.

Anyeta's admonition to most young girls who sought her advice on illnesses, including pains in the stomach and fainting fits, was to tell them that they were not eating correctly. "Do not eat so much meat, take more vegetables, especially the *purum*, the onion, young lady, and you will feel better."

We Romanies ate mainly stews which in the old days we made in a pot over a fire. With the arrival of the vardo in the mid-eighteen hundreds we began to cook on stoves and our dishes gradually became more sophisticated, but by no means more delicious.

In Canada, when I was training with
the RAF, during the war

A home on wheels – a typical gipsy vardo

The Romany Boy

A typical stew made over the camp fire would be fried meat and potatoes with plenty of onions, topped up with water and as many varied herbs as could be gathered. Last were added the greens so that they would be crisp to eat. I believe the Italians call it *al dento*. Chewy might be the word. Sometimes we would make dumplings of flour and egg and water or of oatmeal and suet together with the blood of the meat. Herbs were often added to the dumplings, too.

The herbs used in my mother's cookery were the usual garden ones. She could buy them from local shops or sometimes she was given them by a local farmer's wife. If my father had decided to park the vardo in one place for more than six months, she would grow her own in pots and boxes from seed.

My favourite was sage. "Sage," my father said, in one of his mealtime monologues (my mother was not a talker and I was too busy stuffing my mouth full of delicious food to *rokker* much), "Sage helps to kill the poisons in meat. Then your liver won't have to work hard producing the antidotes. Thyme will bring out the virtues of foods and it prevents your belly being blown out with wind. As for rosemary," he'd continue, "that is indeed a wonderful little herb for it will fight water retention in the body and it's very effective when it's used with marrow or tomatoes. And if you want to keep young, Lion, always eat some marjoram."

My mother used herbs with a delicate touch, and they were never overpowering in her cooking.

Although I would rarely eat hedgehog because of my love for Spike (whom my mother disliked because, as you know, hedgehogs are full of fleas), I watched Anyeta and my cousins' tribe kill and eat one on several of my visits.

They killed the animal with a sharp blow to the nose—for a hedgehog this is instant death—and allowed the blood to drain, then burned off the bristles in the fire, and skinned it by cutting along its back and removing the skin in one piece. Then a sharp stick like a skewer was pushed through the carcass lengthways for roasting over the fire; or, if the fire was at the embers stage, the animal was packed in clay before skinning and baked in the ashes. When done the clay was ripped off, taking with it bristles, paws and all, and the meat was then cooked in salted water or roasted.

Another favourite of the gipsies in times gone by was snails. Their more sophisticated relatives 'escargots' on sale in French restaurants, are especially fed on herbs and apples and so have the same delicious taste, but country snails vary according to what food they have been eating. Should they have dined on Deadly Nightshade then they will be poisonous, so the Romanies used to starve the snails for some days before cooking and eating them, or at least they would make sure that they had wholesome food like apple parings.

Anyeta had a recipe for snails as a remedy for bronchitis and chest complaints that my mother memorized just to please her, but I do not think she relished the thought of ever preparing such a concoction.

"Take six or eight snails, put them in a box with some oats, for in walking over this they will rid themselves of slime. Have half a pint of strained barley water boiling and drop the snails in. Then let it all simmer for an hour. Strain it again and put it away, sealed. Add one small spoonful to every glass of liquid that the sick person drinks. It will sooth a cough as sure as the sun do set."

It was amazing that wherever Anyeta travelled word would get around that she was a wise old lady and the country people, themselves rich in folklore, would come to her for advice about the health of their babies or their old folk, or any women's illnesses.

One of her remedies for corns was much sought after. "Gather two or three young ivy leaves, put them in a little jar and cover them with vinegar. This you must leave for a day, fine lady, then cover the corn with one of the leaves and keep it in its place by tying some good gauze around it. You must do this again each day, ever using a fresh ivy leaf." This, if continued for two or three weeks, was said to relieve the pain immediately and later the corn centre would be soft enough to come away.

Anyeta's remedy for chilblains, often suffered by village children who sat in unheated classrooms and then came home to the fire to roast their toes, was to rub on a raw onion dipped in salt; that was if the chilblain was not broken; should it be broken she advised a poultice of hot turnip (baked in the oven until it was soft and then laid in place and tied with a bandage).

The Romany cure-all in any circumstances when I was a child seemed to be the onion. I ate so many that you could perhaps imagine I would get tired of them. Instead, my system became hooked, for if anyone today were to ask me what my favourite meal is I would answer, "A piece of bread and cheese and a raw onion."

Anyeta believed that raw onions cured colds, stopped you from catching influenza, consumption, asthma, ulcers, heart trouble, and who is to say she was not right. If only people had the courage to eat onions raw and stink to high heaven they would be in better health; but such a habit is supposed to be antisocial and I admit that onions should be eaten by everybody present or there is usually hell to pay.

Stronger than the onion is its relative, garlic; again a certain remedial help in circulatory disease, it's invaluable, too, for digestive health. Anyeta loved it, and usually preached its properties for the prolongation of life. To the Romanies it is the herb of old age and wisdom. Anyeta once told me: "Plant a bulb of garlic beneath the rose bush, *chav*, and you'll find it upsets the rose so much that she will give out more scent."

Of all her remedies and recipes Anyeta was most proud of 'Romany Balm', the secret of the Albanian and Romanian Zingaris. One day she drew me aside and told me solemnly

51

that I was to be guardian of the recipe for future generations.

First, Anyeta said, you needed a certain quantity of the fat of the kidneys of a pig. This my father worked out to be approximately four ounces. Then you are to take one ounce or thereabouts of cuttings from the 'frog' of a horse's hoof (these you were quite easily able to obtain from any farrier), one houseleek (the plant that grows on the tiles of cottages and outbuildings) and about one ounce of the scrapings from the bark of the elder tree.

"Place all together in the pot over a low fire, *chav*, and stir while the fat is asizzle, then strain after half the hour has gone by and put into a clean jar. Now this be excellent for any skin places, boils, cuts, sores." And she would tell how a grand lady she knew, having suffered from a skin complaint for nineteen years, had made up the ointment from Anyeta's instructions and cured herself of her trouble where doctors had failed.

For stone in the bladder the herb the Romanies use is gravel root. One ounce boiled in one and a half pints of water for twenty minutes, then strained and bottled. The dose was a small wineglassful taken five or six times a day. Anyeta was never in her life troubled with it, but sympathized when she diagnosed sciatica in others and would pass on this remedy: "Do you take one ounce of the herb ragwort in one pint of water, missus, as if you be making tea, then strain, and you can take a little bit three times a day and it will help to chase away the ache."

Cystitis she cured with parsley-piert. One ounce boiled for a minute in a pint of water, strained and taken once a day in a wine glass. Another good herb for this condition was couch-grass root. She would boil one ounce in one and a half pints of water for five minutes before straining and bottling. The dose was a wineglassful five times a day.

Her own ministrations to me when young were few because, fortunately, I was a healthy child, afflicted only by the few ills

I caught from classmates. Whooping cough she 'cured' with the herb mouse-ear, and once when I had been greedy and was bilious, she dosed me with an infusion of spearmint three times a day.

The flowers of the cowslip were her standby for a good night's sleep – not that many travellers suffered this way, being usually ready to sleep as soon as their heads were down. She infused the flowers as you would tea, setting the liquid to stand for five minutes, and then added a little milk.

My favourite remedy was Anyeta's cough medicine, which tasted pleasant and was effective enough. I even used to simulate a cough in order to be given some; yet she always knew the true from the false, and on the occasions I was cheating studiously ignored my hacking groans.

She told Marie the ingredients needed for the medicine: a quarter of a pint of white vinegar, two ounces of honey, a quarter of an ounce of black liquorice, and one lemon. She was to place the vinegar and the finely chopped liquorice in a basin and place this in a very hot oven and stir occasionally until the liquorice dissolved. Then the honey was to be added, followed by the juice of a lemon. The dose was about a teaspoonful when the cough was troublesome.

Anyeta's own preventative of colds on the chest was efficient as far as I know, for she had no trouble with the common scourge. In winter she would rub an ordinary tallow candle on a piece of coarse brown paper, then place this, greased side next to the skin, under her clothes, over her back and chest. No wind could penetrate this. Pieces of this greased paper cut to the shape of the foot were often worn by gipsies inside their shoes to keep out the damp.

Of all the herbs in the world the one that really scared the wits out of me was mandrake, for it has a root in the shape of the human body, with legs and arms and head, and when you pulled it from the ground it shrieked in agony. Anyeta was always on the lookout for mandrake because it is a good cure

53

for chest troubles and she was able to sell it to herbalists. There is a male plant and a female; both send their vine-like feelers along the ground until they meet, then they tighten and intertwine until the two roots draw close together and touch when, it is said, they mate. Strange lovers. As a plant the mandrake really is an uncanny freak of nature.

There seemed to me, as a child, to be no end to Anyeta's wisdom. She knew enough to fill several books—chestnut poultices for piles; a chestnut leaf syrup for chestiness; a herbal tobacco for asthma; alder berries for constipation; stinging nettle tea for high blood pressure; hedgehog fat for deafness; hedgehog fat and St John's Wort for preventing baldness; elder flowers, peppermint and yarrow tea for a cold.

She was always brewing, always mumbling incantations over her brews and always ready with good advice. She also knew what was to come.

One day she said to me: "Now, *chav*, I wish you have listened to all I *pookered*, for it will be not more than a moon (month) and I shall *jal avree* (go away), for I am *poori* (old). And when I go I shall *coor the drom* for the last time to the *Kooshti Duvel* above."

She was as good as her word. In a month she was dead and my father and his cousins mourned her with *bosh* and *gilli* (fiddle and song). She had a Christian burial at which all her friends in life were present.

Anyeta had lived a long time and spoken words of wisdom to gipsy and *gorgio* alike until at last she found her final *atchen tan* (stopping place). And for me she left a good *pateran* to show the way. I will never forget her and the wisdom of her ways.

Anyeta's death was, despite her great age, traumatic for me. I had thought she would go on forever; it seemed perfectly natural that she should have some secret magic, some potent potion, perhaps, which would make her eternal.

She was the first human being I saw after death, and I was shocked into a kind of awe for the power of the spirit to invest a human being's body with its true life, to create the impression of power and youth.

Anyeta alive had been a vigorous, vital woman for her age (and she was over eighty when I knew her). Anyeta dead was, I thought, like the gnarled trunk of a fallen tree. Had she ever spoken, laughed, twinkled at me in humour, flashed me looks of scorn when I was ignorant or bad? It was hard to believe that she had.

My grandmother was laid out by *gorgios*. For we Romany people are not inclined to relish the prospect of handling the dead. Modern gipsies do not like to be reminded that many of their number have been buried in the past in unsanctified ground, but this does seem to be so. For instance, the Herons, Grays, Smiths and Youngs certainly buried many of their dead up on 'Mussel'—Mousehold Heath near Norwich, and it does seem natural that their dead should be buried almost where they fell, by the wayside, yet nearly a hundred per cent of gipsies profess themselves to be Christian, and their preference is for a Christian burial in sanctified ground, albeit as near the hedgerow of a churchyard as possible!

Anyeta had told Xavier that she wished to be buried in a piece of land adjoining the churchyard. There was to be no name engraved on stone above the grave, but the grass and wild flowers were to be allowed to grow unhindered over the place. She called tombstones 'the stones of mockery'. She said the *gorgio* fought and quarrelled and hated in life and then thought all could be smoothed away in death by a lying epitaph. She would rather have her name engraved on the warm hearts of those she loved, she said, than etched in cold stone.

Before she died Anyeta had held many small conferences with Xavier, talking to him about the past from where she lay, her hand in his. She gave him back all the money he had ever given her as a dutiful son as part of his earnings in youth. She gave him a present of some fine shirts that she had made, embroidered in the Romanian style, and she gave him her jewels, which she had bought through the years with her savings.

In his writings my father always spoke of himself as being single at the time of Anyeta's death; but this, in fact, was artist's licence. Marie and I were certainly sharing his life by then, but he had transposed Anyeta's death to an earlier time, not so much an inaccuracy, perhaps, as a 'rearrangement'.

Anyeta gave Xavier one last present, the date of his death, which she predicted as 1949. She was too early. Xavier died in 1957.

Her message to Xavier was: "Always be straight, pet. Look at the ones who are not and see what a mess they made of it. A man with an uneasy conscience is like a bee in a syrup jar. The more he flies about the more he glues his wings up."

She was full of such cryptic and wise sayings. "Don't apologize if you are not sorry."

"Remember that a hypocrite is always worse than a rogue."

"A kind word can unlock a cold heart quicker than a gold klizina."

"Hard hearts are good in cabbages but not in people."

And once, when Xavier complained that he'd got the blame for something he hadn't done and had even helped the person concerned by curing an ailment, she said: "Never mind, pet, the best man who ever lived was crucified. And He'd raised the dead."

Of character she said: "Leather is best when it has had a good hammering." She believed in life's knocks for character forming.

And before she left us she gave to Xavier all her secrets: the secret of the Tarot cards, and she gave him her treasured pack; the magic of the number twenty-six derived from the *Yod-he—vau-he*, most mysterious of all words to which she gave Xavier, her son, the key; and the eye-tooth of her father, Zig. This last would charm away warts, but Xavier was never to take payment for such a service. The eye-tooth, sacred among the Zingaris, Xavier told me, is regarded as a sacred trust, for in parting with it the true *Rom* gives over into your keeping his knowledge, his gift of prophecy, and his power over the future.

True to Anyeta's wish, her burial was carried out in simple fashion. She had for some months been out of her vardo, and lying in a room of a *gorgio's* house, for this friend had wished to save her life; so there was no *vardo* now to be *yagged*, no possessions left in it to burn. She had handed everything over to her heirs before her death, breaking with tradition, but apparently unafraid to do so, for in her view it would have been a colossal waste to burn her home and all her treasured possessions.

The coffin of Anyeta was left open for several days after her death so that all her relatives and even *gorgio* friends could see her and pay their last respects, and only when all were gathered from every part of the country, was the coffin closed. This has long been a custom among the Romanies, and yet it is recorded that, "when Lawrence Boswell's eldest son, Moses, died at Etwall, near Derby in 1855, his widow Trenit Heron, excluded visitors from the 'death tent', and even refused to allow relations to view the body. The East Anglian Smiths and Browns, the latter being Herons under an assumed name, secreted their dead in the same manner, according to Katie Smith, a granddaughter of 'Jasper Petulengro'."

Most bereaved Romanies fast while their dead lie unburied; at least red meat is barred, and sometimes the eating of all cooked food. This fast is broken by the feast on the day of the burial which is no mean affair and is not undertaken at a time of sadness—the sadness being over—but a time of rejoicing to speed the dead on their way to Paradise.

True to tradition, Xavier watched over Anyeta's body after death and up to the time of her burial. This vigil is a very long established custom among all gipsies. In many cases the corpse is illuminated by candles at the head and feet during this time of mourning.

Anyeta was buried in her best clothes, but without her shoes, and round her waist she wore a belt decorated with silver trinkets—and with pockets in which money had been placed.

Most gipsies go to their burial place fully dressed, with perhaps a spare set of clothes and some other personal possessions in their coffin. My father followed Anyeta's wishes in not including her shoes, for it was not the custom of her tribe to do so, yet there have been cases where gipsies were buried in their silver buckle shoes.

One was Louis Boswell who died in 1839. He was fully dressed and wore buckle shoes; in his pockets were watch, pocket-knife, and money, beside him his walking stick, silver tankard and fiddle. And when his daughter Vashti died later the same year, she, too, wore silver-buckled shoes; but this is a custom which was confined mainly to gipsies in the Midlands. My father's people, from Wales and East Anglia, did not follow the custom of their cousins.

Thompson, the gipsy-lore historian, records that Ethelenda Heron was buried with her entire wardrobe, and the same goes for Santinia Smith. Savinia Lovell was placed in the coffin with two dresses and a silk shawl and other 'bits o' finery'. But all these were buried in their undergarments, the finery being laid beside them.

There were two differing beliefs on this. Some gipsies believed in burial in clothes, but no additions or accessories in the coffin, nor was any kind of headgear worn—although Eliza Heron was said to be buried in Norfolk in 1887 'in a scarlet bonnet'. Other tribes believed in including all sorts of loose articles in the coffin. Yet, although the East Anglian gipsies buried their dead in clothes and disapproved of separate inclusions, it was said that Elizabeth Smith was buried with two fine Brussels carpets at her side, 'one large', as well as the strip on which she was laid out.

At Anyeta's graveside my father stood with tears rolling down his face, and before the first clod of earth was thrown, he tossed a golden sovereign into the depths and onto the coffin.

It was his farewell gesture of love and respect to the woman who gave him life.

6

Shooshies and Gryes and the Like

A *shooshie* is a rabbit; a *grye* is a horse. Both animals are important to the Romany, the horse for transport and as an article of sale, the rabbit not so much for food as for its skin. Xavier loved to quote the wise old saying (though I'm sure he made it up): "There are two foods a Romany distrusts: the sausage and the rabbit. The sausage, because he doesn't know enough about it. The rabbit because he knows too much."

My own poaching days were over soon, cut short by the war and service with the RAF. After a spell killing for king and country, I had no heart on my return to peacetime life to kill wild things and ever since have chosen to live and let live.

Not so Xavier; reared in harsher times he knew all the poaching skills and used them. I describe them here as part of the Romany way of life, but must say that I no longer indulge myself in this kind of 'sport'. The killing of animals sickens me and meat is not my favourite food.

Xavier had a double-barrel shotgun, but seldom used it. As he had to carry out most of his expeditions after game as furtively as possible, it would have been far too noisy a weapon for his purpose, so he kept it mainly for the killing of crows and other carrion.

Should he wish to use the gun on rabbits he had a method of making them come to him which worked very well. He would mix together oil of parsley, oil of angelica, oil of aniseed and oil of copaiba, place it on twigs or pieces of wood, then put them in a field and wait for the animals (rabbit or hare) to appear.

For getting rabbits or rats from burrows he used a method which he taught me. We cut coarse brown paper in strips about eighteen inches by two inches, then we made up a solution of saltpetre, Cayenne pepper, and enough vinegar to make it like paste. This we brushed over the paper strips which we then dried and rolled up. We placed them in a hole on the windward side and set them alight; then we'd place a piece of turf over the fire when it was going well. Having first placed a net over the other entrance to the burrow, we could wait in confidence for the doomed animal to emerge.

I discovered early on that I had no killer instinct, but I did not mind in the least helping to cure the skins of the dead animals. First we would stretch out the pelt and nail it down to a piece of wood, then scrape off as much of the fatty inner skin as we could, using a blunt knife for the job. Xavier had already mixed a solution of eight ounces of alum powder with two pints of boiling water and we would rub this all over the inside of the skins, leave to dry and then repeat. Next we boiled a handful of oak bark in a quart of water; with this we washed the inside of the skin. The whole operation could take a week.

When he was satisfied with the condition of the pelt my father would untack the skin and rub in two ounces of olive oil and two ounces of linseed oil to make the pelt supple. We then laid the skin on a sheet of brown paper, fur uppermost, and dusted this with a mixture of one ounce of alum and one ounce of bitter apple. After it had been left for a couple of days the fur was brushed and the pelt rubbed to make it supple.

"We Romanies don't like shot in our *shooshies*," Xavier used to say, "and that's why we never use a gun."

If we were near a warren our sense of smell told us whether or not Mr *Shooshie* was at home. When the hole was empty it gave off a cold, damp smell. But if the rabbit was at home it gave off a warm smell like 'a litter of puppies', as my father declared.

The morning I learned from him the gipsy method of trapping a hare, the grass was still drenched in dew. We sat on a gate chewing a blade each and looked through the morning haze at the water meadows which stretched away to where some willows marched along the banks of a tributary of the Cam.

"Sally the *caneegra* always runs in tracks across the field." Here began the first lesson. "She makes the road herself and can find her way across a field to her home again as quick as a flash, so we must be quick, too. Remember this: as she runs she looks back over her shoulder.

"Now! To see whether a hare still uses a road—like the one I showed you—we must set a gager." Xavier cut pieces of bramble stick from the hedgerow and set them about three feet apart in the grass across the tracks, then withdrew to our vantage point.

"Now, Lion, the Sally, who knows her road by heart, will run with her eyes looking backwards and will bump into the gager as she goes, disturbing it and leaving us our clue, boy."

He slapped me on the back—the sign to get up and go. We went our way through the neighbouring field back to the vardo, the dew-soaked grass slapping and squelching under our tread.

Sure enough, the next day the bramble sticks were covered in tiny clusters of fur. Without disturbing the sticks, we set our snare three or four yards further along—a snare made of five strands of brass wire. The end was looped and from it Xavier hung a pail, revolving it so that it twisted the strands of wire perfectly to make a solid plait. The pail was removed and the end of the wire placed through the loop. Then the snare was set in the grass on the road, clear of the bramble sticks that Sally the *caneegra* would follow.

"She'll be in the noose before she knows anything," my

father assured me, "for knowing she was pricked by some enemy the night before, she'll run to one side of the road, looking behind all the time for the unknown . . ."

We returned to the spot the next morning and there I saw the beautiful animal, ensnared. Dead, but not without struggle, obviously. I had no sentimental feeling for dead things; I did not as a child feel repugnance at killing, but when I imagined the struggles of that beautiful beast I vowed never again to trap a hare. And I never did.

Some mornings later I almost stepped on its twin. I was out early—without Rufus the collie, this time—down by the river and just as I was about to step on it, I saw the hare in front of me. It was 'frozen' in its set, a motionless thing of beauty; obviously it had been surprised by my appearance and, rather than make a run for it, had chosen to stay moulded to the earth in the hope that I would overlook it. It was the colour of the earth, a lovely reddish mud brown.

I walked on and never told my father.

The horse or *grye* is an important part of Romany folklore. We were ever an independent people and considered ourselves to be traders rather than beggars. Whether we carried our wares from door to door, or travelled over all Europe, as my grandfather did, trading horses, we were proud of our powers as salesmen and saleswomen, and nothing pleased us better than to bring off a deal.

From an early age I learned the value of barter or *chop* as an alternative to a sale brought off by exchange of money.

In fact, I am sure that the former was more pleasing to us. Many a time as a boy my father came home from peddling wares with his pockets full of eggs, pickles and cheese rather than money, and these were not spurned at all, for they were good to eat and coppers are not. In the country lanes and at cottage doors he learned how to tell if a woman had any money or not; it was something of an instinctive guess, rather than a calculated deduction, but if she kept chickens, well, eggs would do instead of silver. Even I, in time became expert at assessing the value of a piece of cloth or a clock in eggs or goat's cheese.

Now, when it comes to trading horses, a Romany must be skilled and knowing, and he usually is. Not that he expects to do any *gorgio* down; it is more likely, in his opinion, that the *gorgio* will cheat him. When up against his own kind the Romany must be cunning too, for here is an adversary worth having.

Every deal that my grandfather made was clinched with a special handshake; no written contract was needed, for, of course, he couldn't write. But his word was his bond. Indeed, as Xavier used to sing:

> *You can trust a Romany for your best friend,*
> *You can trust a Romany to the end,*
> *He won't rob you, he won't lie,*
> *You can trust him till you die;*
> *But, hate him, and you'll come off worse,*
> *For he can haunt you with a curse!*

A horse to a Romany is not *mokado*—unclean—as is the dog. He is a friend; you'll never see a gipsy of true Romany descent maltreating a *grye*.

The typical gipsy pony is a skewbald of sturdy stock, but to pull his vardo Xavier had two bays almost as big as Suffolk Punches, and he treated them well, for in hilly country he would always hire two from a farm to help get the huge Pullman up hill and down dale.

The name *grye-kopers* in Romany means horse-keepers, and down the years the *kopers* became the Coopers. There are many Romany families who travel under the name of 'Grey', a form of grye. and it is from this that I derive one of my names, 'Lloyd', for lloyd in Welsh means grey. My second surname, and the one by which my family is best known

comes from *petul-engro*, horseshoe-maker—so my family link
with horses is double-forged.

My grandfather I know (though I don't remember him
clearly) was one of the greatest of all horse dealers and a
legend in his lifetime. He could take an animal in at a glance,
without turning his head or looking askance, but by staring
straight ahead and looking, so to speak, out of the corner of
his eye. (It's a well-known talent of the Romanies and was of
great help to me in my days as an air gunner in the RAF.)
He would appear not to be very interested in an animal when
making a deal, hardly giving it a glance, but knowing all the
time what good or bad points it had.

He went to fairs in Wales, at Barnet, all over Kent and
Surrey and travelled through Europe as far as Romania,
where, of course, he had met Anyeta. He knew all the dates of
all the auctions all over Britain, though he could not read or
write, and was known and trusted everywhere.

Xavier inherited his father's instinctive talents but not his
zeal, his time being mainly taken up with salesmanship in the
early years and, later, with showmanship, when he toured the
country with his gipsy band and variety show in the 'forties
and 'fifties.

I have one vivid memory of attending a sale with my father
when I was about ten years old. We were up early on this
particular morning and off to catch the train to London and
then out to Barnet by Underground. We travelled by train
when we had to go any distance, for a short time in those
days, and it was always a very rare treat for me.

Our food was wrapped for the journey by my mother, in
waxed paper and a cheese-cloth. It consisted of goat's cheese,
home-made bread, apples and a honeycomb. Our hearts were
merry as, after a cold, grey dawn, the sun appeared around
ten o'clock as we were approaching the fair. We walked from
the station, trudging in company with dozens of others, many
of whom Xavier knew and called greetings to.

The music reached us first, then, round a bend in the road we could see the fair; a blaze of tents and moving figures, and the adjoining funfair had already started taking in paying customers. You could sniff the salty smell of horses half a mile away.

Xavier wandered through the crowd, patting a pony's nose, feeling the fetlock of a huge Shire, turning away sadly from a sway-back gelding, slapping the neck of a sturdy Welsh pony. He knew exactly what he was looking for because a retired naval captain, a long-standing friend from Long Melford, had asked him to find an animal that would fit his requirements. It was to be a hack for his twelve-year-old daughter, preferably a bay or a roan—for greys were thought to be unreliable—of fourteen-and-a-half hands, healthy, with no flaws, pretty into the bargain, with some distinguishing feature such as a white flash.

I sensed his excitement when we had been at the fair a half hour. He had found the animal he wanted, but the farmer who was selling, a rough and ill-natured character with a red face, hardly seemed likely to let the animal go at a low price. Xavier knew he must hurry, or a pretty little roan filly like that would soon be snapped up.

"Good-day, sir," Xavier said, taking a step towards this adversary and saluting. "That's an interesting animal. How much for her?"

"Hmph," snapped the farmer, eyeing Xavier's gold-braided bolero, his scarf knotted at his throat, his gold sleepers in his ears, the trews with flashes of red satin. "Hmph." Then he took a second look at my father's broad shoulders and appeared slightly less fierce. "She's not for the likes of you, gippo. Too delicate a creature to pull your caravan."

"Ah, sir," said Xavier, keeping his temper. "I have my own good *gryes* for that, thank you. No, this young 'un will be only employed to carry a young lady, light as a bird. How much? I see, by-the-by, you have no bridle on her. Is she broken yet?"

"She's broken all right," said the farmer, "or why else do you think she be a-standing here like a lady at court? No. I don't have to bother with a bridle, so gentle is she. But how do I know you're serious about the young lady who'll ride her. How do I know you're telling the truth?"

My father produced a letter from his pocket. The address was a good one, the signature educated. The letter spoke of the buyer's intent, and named Xavier as agent. There was only one disadvantageous thing about the letter; obviously someone of substance was after the little horse, and therefore the farmer might not drop his price.

Xavier, however, was a solid match for him. They bargained and hassled for a full hour before the deal was clinched, but Xavier walked away from the fair that evening with a prize, a roan filly for seven pounds.

That night we slept at an inn that had stabling, and I lay awake thinking about the little horse in the shed. In all my eleven years on earth my father had never let me have a horse of my own, and I envied the young lady who was to have her. There was just one magical moment to the whole trip; for an hour Xavier let me ride the filly on our route home, but after that we walked at her side, taking secondary roads and by-ways, so as not to tire her with the noise of traffic. It took us three days to reach the wilds of Suffolk once more, and one night was spent camping in a field.

The little horse reached Long Melford, none the worse for wear, for Xavier had been careful not to overstretch her on the journey.

I often heard of her after that at the local hunt, but I would not become a spectator to her hunting prowess, and never went to watch the hunt in action as my mother did. Perhaps I was just jealous.

For true gipsies the horse is almost a sacred animal. Their

ancient, greeting: "May your horse live long," reflects their reverence for this beautiful animal. Nor will a gipsy ever eat horseflesh. When a *grye* dies it is buried and no predator would be allowed near the carcass.

In spite of this it's strange to think that the gipsies, though excellent horse breeders and dealers, were never very excellent or daring horsemen, as were the Cossacks or the Mongolians of the great Eastern plains. Xavier, in fact, sat a horse badly; Marie was the better rider. And I'm sorry to tell that Xavier was not always kind, just as his ancestors had that cruel streak when it came to horse-dealing. I remember once when a large stubborn *grye* refused to budge, Xavier gathered hay to light a fire underneath the reluctant beast. He never got as far as lighting the intended conflagration because the *grye*, prompted by some horsy instinct, started to move at long last. Not that Xavier would ever beat or starve a *grye*! It was merely that he knew and approved all the old gipsy tricks for showing a horse off at a fair.

Shaking a pail full of pebbles under the animal's nose until it was almost driven crazy by the noise was a common trick. This would make it appear a very spirited animal when the time came for the sale, for the mere sight of a bucket would start it high-pacing, prancing and shaking its mane.

My father was a good horse doctor, a skill which he did not pass on to me. Indeed I have unfortunately been little in touch with horses, living in the age of the motor car.

I remember he always used to tell the story of how he had cured a farmer's horse of some malady with special tablets and, watching the horse galloping round the field after several days of treatment, the farmer had turned to him and said: "Now me owd boy, do you be giving us some o' they tarblets so's we do catch up wi' that owd horse."

"And," said Xavier in concluding his tale," he would have taken them, too!"

Today the Romany is not so much involved with the horse

as with its successor, the motor car, and many of them have
become second-hand car-dealers or breakers and scrap
merchants.

7

Romany Rommerin

The journey to the Romany *rommerin* (wedding) of my second cousin, Mat Lovell, was begun on a fine May morning when I was eleven. I remember the shine of the morning, the shallow slant of the sun as we set off for the festivities along the lanes of Suffolk and out into the flatlands of Norfolk, across the heath towards the woodlands where the happy deed was to take place.

The *gryes* were clip-clopping sturdily as the sun rose in the sky, pulling the vardo at a steady pace. My mother travelled ahead in her gig, the collie lay on the steps with my father and me as we drove the *gryes* along the way.

My parents looked fresh and sprightly, yet Marie had been up half the night packing away the breakables, storing the heavy stuff in the kettle-box slung at the rear of the vardo and seeing to it that we had our contribution towards the *habben* (feast). Xavier had taken the *gryes* to the smithy for some work on their shoes, and I had been sent running on a dozen errands, at anyone's beck and call.

It was a late spring and the first unfurling green of hawthorn was now in evidence, followed soon by birch and elm, ash and oak. The hedgerows sparkled with starry stitchwort and celandine; a wren trilled a cascade of silver notes and over a distant meadow the lark rose, proclaiming its joy in living.

I for one, was glad to be on the move. My *gorgio* contacts

with boys my own age were few, but my knowledge of my kind, the Romanies, even less, for the nature of my father's life now took him away from the tribe and I rarely saw them, except on visits or in brief encounters on the by-ways.

Had the journey been a long one we would have travelled by train, leaving the vardo behind, the *gryes* and goats in the care of a farm labourer or joskin, who would be paid well by Xavier for his trouble. We'd take with us our *tans* to pitch alongside others at the site of the Romany *rommerin*. But this journey was no more than seventy miles and easily managed over the gentle undulations of Suffolk and the flatness of the Norfolk and Lincolnshire lands.

Travelling long distances by vardo was becoming altogether less frequent, and we never travelled during the winter. That was when we rested and reshod the horses, repaired and painted the vardo, and generally took stock of our possessions. It was in winter time that Xavier thought up his new schemes, such as his role as *mug-fakir*.

It was during the long winter evenings, too, that we cleaned the gig and all the brasswork on the horses' harnesses until it shone like the stars and moon, and the black leather horse collar was made to shine like black patent. In winter, in the early days of my childhood I remember Marie, making baskets, pegs, lace and artificial flowers, while Xavier did wood-carving, made jewellery from his knowledge of metal work, and strung all manner of beads.

Xavier could always make an extra bob or two grinding knives, sickles, axes and shears. I know that many Romany travellers helped the farmers with hedging, ditching and pest control, although Xavier seldom joined in these activities in my lifetime, apart from the gathering of herbs, wild flowers such as the dandelion and cowslip for wine, and stinging nettles for medicines that according to him would cure anything. This, however was a spring activity.

Now, on this fine morning, the winter was just a memory.

The whole of the summer lay ahead, with all its scents and sounds, and I could feel the sap rising in me like an excitement as we did *coor the drom*.

I thought with a thrill about my best *togs* hanging beside those of my parents in the vardo, swinging as we travelled, on their wire hangers. (Yes, my father invented the wire hanger for us long before it became a commercial throw-away item.) I thought about my long trews, with leather insets near the hem, my silk shirt of yellow and the red brocade bolero with gold and black braided edges, stitched by Marie, and jingling now with brass sequins. The scarf for my throat was pure silk, too, in a fair paisley design, bought in a shop ready-made with money! My shoes were black with silver buckles.

Xavier was to wear his black Zingari trews and boots and the black velvet bolero embroidered with real gold thread, with tassled epaulettes and a cream silk shirt with Hungarian sleeves. His moustache shampooed and waxed carefully for the occasion, his black hair wrapped in a scarf of red silk, he was aware that he would be the centre of all eyes, for he was going to conduct the Zingari ceremony.

Marie was the least resplendent, but the most beautiful of the three of us. For the *boro divvas* (great day) tomorrow, she would put on her two cambric petticoats, the black skirt with red braiding, the red velvet bodice, cross-laced over a white embroidered blouse, and she would pile her corn-coloured hair on top of her head, before putting on the shawl of brilliant embroidery edged with silvery tinkling sequins.

The journey took two days. We reached the site of the *rommerin* long after sunset on the second day, which was at eight thirty, it being summer time, not Greenwich time. We could hear the noise of *bosh* and laughter and see the glow of the great *yag* long before we actually came upon the scene.

Xavier hailed Maska, his cousin and father of the bride-groom, and a great shout went up when our vardo was sighted. A crowd of Romany *roms* and *juvals*, *chals* and *chis*, came streaming towards us, took our hands in greeting. The dogs barked, Rufus replied with a great commotion and immediately started a fight with one skinny looking lurcher of that company, from whom he had to be torn away before he was demolished.

The scrap over, we were helped to position the vardo in our place among the great circle of vehicles around the fire, and this achieved we sat down to a good meal and gossip.

Maska offered my father some of his home-brewed *kini*, the special gipsy wine that is very potent, but not as potent as my father once inadvertently made out, for while spelling out the recipe in all its stages for a lady journalist, he said: "Bung tightly and stand aside;" as if it were indeed capable of going off with a bang.

In the darkness by the leaping light of the flames, with a small mug of *kini* inside me, I began to enter into the spirit of things. The children my own age gathered round to talk, the *chals* sizing each other up, the *chis* giggling and looking askance, their dark eyes sparkling in the glancing light of the flames.

My second cousin, Manfri, was a year older than I and slightly taller, but not so broad in the shoulders. Realizing I was what he considered easy prey he began to needle me in a not very subtle way.

"Well then, Romany *chal*, you be agonna see a *rommerin* for the first time in your life. Don't stick with no tribe do 'ee for I've heard Maska tell of how you *rokker* more *kant* than Romany, and how you are friends with the *plastramengros* and if that be true you ain't no *pral* of *memo* (no brother of mine)."

He sneered. For the moment I kept cool, though I could feel my blood rising in my cheeks. The *chis* were watching me and I could sense the eyes of one of them on me. I had noticed her when we first drove into the clearing in the wood where the moon now shone full on the scene. For a while now I hesitated.

"As for Xavier, he who calls himself a *Rom*, he be nothing but a *wafodi moosh*, a *potrash*, who has left our *kooshti* ways of *grafting* (a bad man, a half-breed who has left our good ways of working) and is nothing better than a *moocher* (beggar)."

He let out a scornful laugh and had I been older I would have thought it theatrical, but at the time I was overcome with rage and humiliation. This I could not allow. He had deliberately blackened my father's name. And none of it was true. Obviously Maska was jealous of Xavier who was now head of the tribe, a Prince, after Anyeta died.

Then I went for him with my *maulies* (fists), aimed at the jaw with my right, a true long melford, as my father had taught, then followed up with a left, right, left, like the drumming of a *shooshie* on his chest. He came back with a right hook, then a straight left, but was wide open for my upper cut and toppled back against the wheels of a vardo.

The watchers had gathered into a circle, the *chis* wide-eyed, the *chals* calling encouragement to Manfri. Lying on the ground he snarled at me with all the ferocity of an angry gorilla, for I thought he looked like one.

"You *melali joobli minj*," he screamed as he staggered up, and although it may sound like Goon language today, I assure you that he was being very rude, not in true Romany, but in didikai slang. He lowered his head like a bull and came at me. Swift as a matador I stepped aside then smartly kicked him in the rear. He turned and we grappled, rolling over and over on the woodland floor towards the flames of the *yag*. By that time the *chis* were screaming, the *juggals* barking and there was a fine old *chingary*.

That's strange, I thought, as I felt the drenching patter of rain, I had not seen a single cloud warning of *parni*. But this *parni* came from buckets and I rolled away from Manfri and gazed up at the grinning circle of faces, one of whom I recognized as belonging to my father.

"Come along, Lion," he said, hooking me to my feet by the

scruff. "We'll have no more *chingary*; you can forget all this. Now shake hands with your cousin and let's *avree* to the *vardo* before you do any more damage." I could feel the trickle of blood on my cheek, but was gratified to see on Manfri's countenance the beginnings of a beautiful black eye.

We shook hands, grinning. Friends now; no more would be said. We had settled our argument in the honourable way and proved our Romany blood, but I could see the girl with the white skin and dark eyes looking at me proudly as if I were the victor. I did not smile at her but moved sternly away. After all, to smile at an admiring female would be a sign of weakness.

Her name was Starella, as I soon discovered when the encampment had risen for the coming day's festivities. The sun was just up, the morning chorus had begun long before the dawn at four o'clock, and although I was not used to the woodland birds, I could recognize a thrush and blackbird, nuthatch and robin.

Starella was already dressed in her best when I saw her; velvet, silk and silver tassels. She looked, I thought, more beautiful than my mother, with *lulagis* (flowers) in her hair. She had a fiery and foreign look to me, and I had a strange sensation in my chest, which was new to me. Not even Mary-Anne, in that fated classroom, had made me feel like this.

I made the first overture and learned that her name was Wood. She was the granddaughter of a famous horse breeder and dealer and had true Zingari blood in her veins. Her dark hair had a sheen like that on a black *grye's* flank, I thought, for want of a better comparison. I had yet to hear of ravens' wings in that context.

She told me that she was twelve years old and one of the maids at the wedding ceremony. I told her that I was thirteen, and the son of Xavier Petulengro. Both pieces of information, one a lie, one the truth, seemed to impress her greatly.

All morning of the *boro divvas* the women were working, raking up the great fire, ready for the *baulo cirol* (pig roasting). The *Roms* put out the beer in the shade of the trees and great kegs of *kini* were brought from many vardos, too. All the morning long poor Matt, the bridegroom, was the butt of jokes and innuendoes, and had to undergo the indignity of having beer poured over his naked chest, all part of the ritual.

By afternoon all was ready. The *boas-venos* (fiddlers) tuned up, the melodion joined in, and the flute too, with a backing of blackbird, thrush and wren.

At one end of the clearing the *roms* and their wives had built the Romany wedding bower, a wooden arch covered in flowers—apple blossom, mingled with the first rhododendron blossom—wild mauve orchid-like florets. Opposite this glorious sight we, the wedding guests, assembled standing at a distance of about twenty yards.

Xavier, as head of the tribe approached the bower, a resplendent figure in his Zingari *togs*. He was followed by a procession of the bridesmaids, seven young *juvals*, walking after the chief bridesmaid two by two. In their left hand each held a green twig. Three of the bridesmaids carried cushions, another a scarlet cord and two bandages, another, Starella, carried a loaf of bread, and the last two carried each a red cabbage.

Xavier turned and took up his position in the wedding bower, looking more solemn than I had ever seen him, and the bridesmaids formed a semi-circle around him, standing in a horseshoe shape to symbolize the seven nails of the horse-shoe, with its open end towards the company of guests.

There was a hush of expectation as the bridegroom, dressed in his finest *togs* of black braided trews, boots and shirt with silver-buttoned bolero, approached the bower from the right; with him was Hanna, the oldest *juval* of the tribe present. Matt reached the end of the horseshoe of bridesmaids and halted, facing half left.

Now the women let out a gasp of delight as Andrea, his bride, approached with her retinue of Benjamin, the oldest male of the tribe, and two other younger *roms*, in single file. She was dressed in a gold embroidered skirt, white stockings and red high boots, with a gossamer white blouse over which was drawn the most beautiful shawl I had ever seen in my young life. Her red-gold hair was in two braids tied with red ribbon and on her head was a circlet of white orange blossom and lilies-of-the-valley.

When Andrea reached the right end of the horseshoe she halted, turning half right to face Matt. One of the young attendants was carrying a bouquet of wild flowers and herbs, a second a gilded fish and the ring.

The chief bridesmaid stepped forwards as the music faded and there was silence except for the rustle of a small breeze in the trees and the lazy chirrup of afternoon birds. Even the dogs were quiet, lying under the vardos at their stations, and the *gryes*, cropping silently in the next meadow—all but one white arab which was reserved for the bridal couple—were hardly aware of this human ritual to which they had pulled the vardos so many miles.

The chief bridesmaid led Matt by the hand towards Xavier and spoke out clearly for all to hear. "O Chief, I bring to you a true son of the Romany tribe of Lovell, and ask you to wed this Romany to Andrea Boswell by the rites and ritual of the Zingari tribe."

Then the bridesmaid turned towards us and lifted up her arms to heaven as my father rumbled aloud for all the assembled company to hear: "Is there one among you who will not say that this *chal* shall not be *rommered* to Andrea Boswell by the true rites of the Zingari chaleskoe?"

The silence lasted for what seemed an eternity to me. I glanced apprehensively around, wondering who there could be who would speak up now and spoil it all for me, but nobody said anything and I breathed a sigh of relief as one of

77

the young *roms* led Andrea forwards to Xavier, saying: "I, Rolo, bring a true daughter of the tribe of Boswell, and ask you to wed her to Matthew Lovell, by the rites and ritual of the Zingari tribe." Then taking his place beside the bridesmaid he turned to the guests with uplifted arms.

Once again Xavier put the question to the assembly. "Is there one here who will say that this *chi* shall not be *rommered* to Matthew Lovell by the true rite and ritual of the Zingari chaleskoe?"

Again silence, and the two attendants lowered their arms.

Then all the company shouted out: "There is none, my chief, who says these two cannot be *rommered* by the rites of the Zingari and by the mingling of their blood."

Xavier turned to the chief bridesmaid in the bridegroom's retinue and, taking the scarlet cord turned to her and said: "Sister, tie in this cord a knot which is a sign of binding Love." She tied the knot at the end of the cord. Then Xavier approached the second bridesmaid. "Sister, tie in this cord the second knot of Affection." Starella was asked to tie the third knot of Sincerity, the next in line tied the fourth knot of Fidelity, the next the fifth knot of Health, the next the sixth knot of Happiness and the last the seventh knot of Long Life.

This done, Xavier placed the knotted cord in the hands of the first *Rom* attendant, then returned to his place within the horseshoe. Taking Matthew's hand in his, Xavier asked him: "Will you, my son, marry this *chi* according to the laws of the Zingari tribe and swear by the Zingari oath of crossed fingers that you will always love, guard, and protect Andrea, and in times of trouble to aid and support her until life ends? Will you swear that you will never betray her, nor deceive her?"

The bridegroom replied in a firm and deep voice: "All this I swear, my chief. The laws of the Zingari *rommerin* I swear to keep."

Whereupon Xavier turned to the bride and taking her

hand, said: "Will you, Andrea, swear by the laws of the Zingari tribe that you will love and assist in every way to give this man joy and peace? Will you promise to bring up your children in the true Romany way and to abide by your husband's side in happiness, in sickness, or in sorrow. Will you swear that no other man shall ever hold a place in your heart while Matthew breathes and lives on earth?"

Andrea answered: "O chief, I swear by the *Kooshti Duvel* that all this I will do."

I held my breath during the next part of the ritual, for I knew it was now that Xavier was to cut the hands of bride and groom. I watched closely as he took a knife from the elder *Rom* of the tribe and swiftly cut a little knick near the thumb on the left hand of Matthew and in the same place on Andrea's right hand. I could see the blood slowly beginning to trickle over their wrists. Taking once again the knotted silken cord, Xavier tied the two wrists together so that the blood mingled. Then he turned his face to heaven and prayed, in words of his own choice.

"O *Kooshti Duvel*, without whom we have nothing, look down on this *Rom*, Matthew, and this *chi*, Andrea, and bless them and keep them always under the great wing of your love so that they may live out their lives together in happiness, health, and peace."

He took the bouquet carried by one of the attendants, dusted the pollen over the couple to symbolize fertility, handed the bouquet to the bride, and finally cut the silken cord.

The couple parted to allow him to step forwards to speak to the guests.

"I, your chief, pronounce to all who are here assembled that Matthew and Andrea are now one, joined together by the Romany ritual of the mingling of their blood."

At this, Matt and Andrea crossed their forefingers on their foreheads, first his, then hers, then dropped their left hand to their hearts. Xavier then placed the ring on the bride's finger and tied the ribbon on the bridegroom's ear.

The couple embraced and gave the *chumeidai*, the sacred kiss of Marriage.

The bridegroom turned towards the fire and, as the wedding guests drew back, ran forwards and made a great leap over the glowing embers of the *yag* in the centre of the clearing. He turned, waiting for Andrea to follow. She jumped like a deer, holding her skirts as she took a great run at the fire, and sailed over to the cheers of everyone who looked on. Then, with joined hands, they raced together once more towards the *yag* and leapt over. We were still cheering as they cleared the flames easily, showing that they were young and vigorous and would live long lives and that their marriage would prosper.

While we broke ranks and flowed around them, Matthew and Andrea received their first gift from Xavier, bread, which is the symbol of plenty throughout their lives.

One of the young *Roms* led forward the white horse; Matthew jumped astride and pulled Andrea up behind him. Ribbons streaming, their faces alight with happiness, they rode off to their vardo, a discreet meadow away, symbolically to begin their happy life—but I knew that they would be back soon to rejoin the festivities which were due to go on half the night.

As I sought out Starella, I vowed that one day I, too, would marry a Romany *chi* and ride off on a white charger. On that May day it seemed to me the ultimate in all this life could offer.

8

The Elopement

The evening of the *rommerin* was light blue, the air in the clearing filled with smells of roasting meat, potatoes, *kini* and beer. But over all was the pervading scent of summer. The music grew louder, the songs of the younger men bawdier, the cheeks of the bride and groom more flushed and the *chavis* became eventually so excitable that many of them fell asleep through sheer exhaustion.

The dancing and feasting went on until the dusk brought out the first *cherino* of the evening, silver and twinkling its message of peace and hope—a reminder, with its ageless light that had travelled down the centuries to radiate upon our festivities this night, of eternity.

It was dusk and the birds were singing loudly as I crept away from the crowd and went deeper into the trees. Starella and I had arranged to meet in a quiet neck of the woods in order to get to know each other better! Our intentions were strangely innocent by today's standards, or even perhaps by the standards of Merrie England before the dawn of the Victorian gods, who laid down a stricter moral structure for country lasses and lads, by example.

Yet for the Romany, ever a true romantic, ever faithful—never promiscuous if he followed the dictates of his tribe—love was an important event, not to be linked with sex until true maturity, and until the vows which had to be taken could be adhered to as if they were indeed cords of binding love and contentment. I have never known a true *Rom* living the tribal life who was unfaithful to his *juval*, and the same is true of the Romany woman.

My heart, when I arranged to meet Starella deep in the wood that night, was beating with romantic fervour, kindled by the sight of her, and set aflame by yet longer in her company, dancing to the sound of *bosh* and harmonica. My more earthy senses were, strangely, still asleep, and I was not at all interested in doing more than hold her hand or kiss her if she would allow. It sounds virtuous and righteous; in fact it was the way we all lived, respecting our women, admiring, courting with fervour and passion, but not lust. Once married, of course, a Romany *juval* had to work hard and obey her husband, but this arrangement rarely brought as much rowing and disagreement as the normal *gorgio* marriage, and saved a lot of aggravation!

Starella was waiting, sitting in the fork of an oak, and looking down at me with a happy smile. She jumped to the ground and immediately put her arms round me. She smelt of herbs and youth. I on the other hand, knew I smelt of sweat, and regretted it. She kissed me on the mouth.

It was my first kiss from a girl and was nothing like I had imagined. It was more frightening than I had thought and it occurred to me that I was entering an entirely new realm of living. I backed away swiftly from the sensation.

"What be the matter?" she asked. "Do I stink?" Now, I had been deaf before to Starella's rather hard tone of voice, blinded as I was by her dazzling looks. Here, however, I was half aware that it grated upon me.

"No," I said blushing. "You do not. You smell good." I was trying to cope with my reactions and how I wished I had the powers of a poet. For I had nothing to say.

I was confronted with a real live girl of twelve years, with black hair, warm and glowing skin, smiling eyes, luscious mouth, swan-like neck, slim long legs—a classic romantic heroine; and I was not only speechless, but motionless, held in thrall by strange physical vibrations.

A late thrush began its repetitive sweet song and Starella looked sulky as she sensed me listening.

"Good *gow*, *chal*, you be slow and no mistake, for you are standing there like a *dindilo*. I thought we had come here for an *engala* (cuddle). You dinna *rokker* nothing. I thought you were to tell me we'd *coor the drom* to the *boro-gavaste* (big town) and we would be *rommered* and go away for ever."

I looked at her in shock. "But we're too young, Starella." Instant marriage hadn't entered my head. I had just had some vague dream of kisses and courting, and a fair lady to hold in my heart until the day we could ask our parents' permission for the *rommerin*.

It was all happening too quickly for my liking and I picked off a twig and started to chew it thoughtfully.

"What be you doing now? Dreaming? Give me an answer. We can run away together, no matter that we can't be *rommered* yet."

"But that would be against the Romany law," I answered, sure of my facts on that, but ignorant for the moment on the laws of the country.

"Oh, you have no sense, you *dindilo*. You're not at all brave as I thought you were when you were fighting Manfri. You're a coward. Coward."

It was like a little love-affair in a nutshell. The falling in love, the consummation (just one kiss), the innocent hopes (mine), the ambitious plans (hers), the hesitation interpreted as failure (mine), and now her scathing, taunting sarcasm, threatening to emasculate me. I was learning fast the ways of women.

Swept along by the torrent of Starella's passion for adventure, I was no more than a twig in the stream, helpless to turn back or to control my destiny in any way. I could feel myself slipping. I knew it was a disastrous thing for me, that my parents would be enraged, that the tribe would censure, that we were too young, that it was insane; yet I gave in.

I was eleven years old and I wanted to appear to be thirteen. I wanted to impress. She saw at once that I had weakened and pounced.

"Do you go on back to vardo now and be as if nothing dinna happen. Then I'll meet you one hour after midnight, here in this place. Bring a *grye* of your Dad's. I seen it cropping in the next field; that's easy—I don' want to fetch away one of ours for they'd see me and wonder what I be up to."

We parted; the lady gave me first a peck on the cheek for my pains, as if to promise something more if I behaved.

My head was a whirl of conjecture as I returned to the festivities in the woodland clearing. What was expected of me? How could I get *dloova* (money) for the journey? I couldn't steal from my father—although taking a *grye* would be a kind of stealing. I began to plan the clothes I'd wear, the food I'd take. I had eleven shillings and fourpence of my own, carefully saved, and I felt sure that this would see us through the first few days.

"Lion! Where have you been, *chal*? Come and help your mother with the *habben* (feast)—there by the *yag*." Marie was taking *puvengras* from the ashes and distributing them with salt and butter; there was a big pot of *cannie* stew bubbling, and the assembled *roms* and *racklers* had brought their own plates for the serving. I joined her and helped to hand out the baked *puvengras*.

The evening dragged by heavily, in spite of the noise and joyful hubbub around me. *Roms* were getting fairly drunk and this had the effect of making the dancing wilder, the *gillies* louder, and the *bosh* faster and faster.

A fight started at about nine o'clock and my father ordered me to bed; but first, he said, I must take his *gryes* to water at the stream.

I crossed two fields to where they grazed peacefully in the grass and whispered to Princess, my father's bay mare, as I haltered her that she was my choice for the night's work. She put up her head and looked down her long nose at me, snickering for titbits, of which I had none.

I patted her flank and with the two other *gryes* haltered, walked to the stream in the other field, then returned them.

In a daze I walked back to the vardo; I could not yet link my decision with reality. Perhaps it was all a dream and I wouldn't have to face the hostile world in the company of this headstrong but beautiful *juval*. Never has there been a more reluctant eloper.

The festivities died down a little near midnight and from my sleeping-bag under the vardo—for the night was warm enough—I heard my parents coming to bed. Rufus was tethered near me and I half wished that I could take him with me, but I knew it would be no good. Just another mouth to feed.

I gave him one last stroke before I crept away at the time I assessed by the moon's position to be midnight, and heard him whimpering softly and pulling at his chain. My luggage consisted of the bridle for the mare and some food in a bundle. Princess nudged me in greeting—I knew her from the white flash on her nose—and I bridled her and led her softly to the place of assignation deep in the wood.

By now I was wishing sincerely that someone would find me or accost me and ask where I was going, but I met no other lovers that night, nor any lurking *chals*. It all seemed to be going against me.

Starella was waiting. "I wondered if you'd come. Why don't you bring the other *grye*? This old mare sure do look slow."

I replied that the mare was more reliable and steadier than the other two. We could both ride her and rely on her not to show temperament.

"What did you bring?" hissed Starella, who had by now

changed out of her finery and was, apart from her splendid boots, in everyday clothes. I, too, had changed into jerkin and leggings and my rough woollen shirt. I showed her the piece of cheese and brown bread together with the two apples that I had knotted in a kerchief. She sniffed.

"I do reckon it'll pass. Look, I have some honey and my mother's white bread and chocolate."

Now chocolate was a luxury I didn't often taste and my mouth began to water.

"Kiss me," demanded Starella, and, trying to put all thoughts of the chocolate out of my head I obliged by giving her one on the lips. I was too agitated to experience once again the turbulence of love I had felt earlier, and snapping, "Quick, or they'll be after us!" scrambled up on Princess's broad back.

"You *dindilo*," whispered Starella from below. "How do you think I be gonna get up there without you to help me? And I do have this blanket to pull across her." I dismounted sulkily, gave her a hand up and then joined her. This put us in the reverse position, she in front and I behind, and I had expected it to be the other way about. She took the reins and when I considered the situation I realized hazily that it was symbolic of our whole pattern of behaviour; she was the leader.

She clucked to Princess, dug her heels in and we were soon trotting and then cantering towards the road.

"Which way to the *boro-gavaste*?" asked Starella. "Have you brought a map?"

"No, we don't have no map. My father do know his way like the lines on his palm."

We cantered across the field, opened a gate and were soon a mile down the road and looking at the first signpost. 'Thetford'. That I knew was on the way to Bury St Edmunds, and from there we could get to Harwich and the boats that went across the North Sea to Holland and Belgium. But Starella was set on going in the direction of Norwich and to

86

Great Yarmouth, where, she said, boats also crossed for the Continent.

We followed the road to Thetford through woods and met only one traveller going in the opposite direction, possibly a forester, who took no notice of us. A car passed us, its headlights carving through the dark, but for the next hour we were alone. We camped that night under some trees in from the road a bit, and woke to hear the dawn chorus as the sun rose.

Starella was up first, her dark hair wild and unbraided. "Mornin' Prince of my heart," she teased, and then looked at Princess where she was tethered. "She do need water soon. We must find a stream."

She opened her bundle of food and started munching. I went off to answer a call of nature behind a tree and thought privately she must be bursting.

Princess was restless and whinnied impatiently, watching Starella pluck bundles of thin grass for her to eat. She talked to the mare soothingly, using a softer tone than she used for me.

Young as we were we'd felt no damp in the night, wrapped up in Starella's blanket, which she had brought rolled up like an Indian's. The dew sparkled and I began to dream as the sun sent fingers of light through the forest.

Starella grinned at me. "Well, *boro rye* (great gentleman), where to next? Eat your breakfast of cheese and brown bread and we'll *coor the drom*." So there was to be no sharing of honey and white bread and chocolate. I ate one of the apples disconsolately and gave the other to Princess.

We rode that morning for hours towards Bungay, for Starella pointed out that it would be better to avoid Norwich on our way to Great Yarmouth. We must follow the river Little Ouse and the Waveney, said Starella importantly, as navigator, and then we would come to Bungay and so to Great Yarmouth.

The morning was bright and the fields by the river hospitable. Opening and shutting gates was my chore. Once we were shouted at by joskins working in the fields, but Princess set off at a good canter leaving them gesticulating on the horizon like little models of men.

With the sun at its height we became hungry. Princess, glad to have us off her back, was watered from the Little Ouse and we began to feel the pains in our stomachs that two healthy adolescents should feel when hunger strikes.

Another hour's walk brought us to the edge of a farmyard. I dismounted and, telling Starella to keep out of sight, gazed over the gate at the few strutting chickens and the couple of geese.

"*Cannies*," hissed Starella, "*cannies* mean eggs, get in and *chorar* some for us." But one look at the two geese told me that I wouldn't get far in my search for the egg boxes that I could expect to find attached to the hen coops—wherever they might be. A skinny *juggal* rushed to the gate and started snarling at me.

"No, I won't steal," I said, bravely turning my back on the dog and its bared fangs. "And I'm not a *moocher* neither, you do it if you do want." Starella could hear the temper mounting in my voice and, woman-like, became immediately soothing. "Oh, now *chal*, no harm meant. What do you think of doing?"

I considered my eleven and fourpence. "We'll go into the next town and pay for our food," I pronounced.

Diss is a pretty town by any standards and in those days it was quiet and tranquil, unspoilt by the railway which the citizens had insisted should be built a mile away. The town clusters round a mere, or lake of about six acres, and this day Starella and I stood looking into its still waters as if we'd find the solution to our problem there. Princess was only interested in drinking the waters.

The people of Diss did not find the sight of us unusual; a

couple of children with a horse. Pony and trap was still a
fairly common form of transport, men still rode about their
farms, and the motor car, which was for the rich, tended then
to be a very unreliable beast, always breaking down and
untrustworthy compared to a good Suffolk Punch or a lively
hack.

We did, however, attract the attention of one person, a
woman, probably the town gossip, who stopped us in the
street and looked at us kindly but speculatively.

"Good arternune. Do yew come from fur? Yew don't come
from these parts. Gippos be yew?"

I nodded. Starella, from her exalted position on Princess's
back, looked scornful.

"I thowt you weresn't from these owd parts," our inquisitor
said triumphantly. "Happen yew be from fur 'cos I never saw
yew afur. Do yew come along of me now, and I do put the owd
Betsy on the fire and yew do sup wi' me."

I took Princess's bridle and made to follow her but was
soon ahead of her. "Now do you wait, young sir, I do be
gettin' into the arternune (getting old) and she there a riding
like a queen," she chortled, jerking her thumb at Starella.

We arrived at her cottage, tied up the *grye* and followed her
indoors. It was dark inside as all old cottages are, for the
windows were small and the panes leaded.

"Do yew be sitting there and sup yar soup," said the old
lady, and placed two bowls in front of us, ladling some good-
smelling stuff from a pot on top of the stove. "Oi' be agonna
out now, but I do be returnin'."

She went out of the door smiling, but I felt uneasy when she
turned the key in the lock after her. We were trapped. The
windows, mullioned, were useless to escape by and the back
door was barred and locked too.

"Oh, eat your soup like a *Rom*," said Starella, "and stop
fussin'."

I tried to obey but I felt that something was wrong. Soon

89

we heard footsteps; two people were approaching the cottage, one was the old lady, the other was obviously a man. We could hear his voice. It seemed to me the man must be a policeman for his voice was deep and authoritative.

"Quick," I whispered to Starella, "get behind the door and when they come in do you bolt through it fast, get to the *grye* and if I don't follow don't wait for me."

The door opened and as he walked in after the old lady I tackled him rugger style as my father had taught me from the side, and shouted to Starella to run—she needed no second bidding. Then I ran through the door and following her, jumped on the back of the *grye* just as she was moving into a trot. We cantered away down the sleepy main street, the centre of a few incurious stares, then made for the open countryside.

"'Course," said Starella, when at last we had our breath back and could speak while Princess was cropping the grass by a stream and we dismounted to drink. "'Course, that waren't no *plastramengro*, that were a parson."

"Parson?" I echoed.

"Yes," Starella chortled with laughter now she felt free, "if we'd stayed, we could ha' been *rommered*."

Still uneasy at these allusions of hers to marriage, and, even now not quite sure what I was doing here on this mad journey, I said merely, "Come on, let's *coor the drom* before the *cherinos* are in the sky. We must find somewhere to sleep."

As twilight was falling we came upon a derelict house. It must have been a beautiful place once, a manor house by its size, but here it was, standing aloof and deserted in its own grounds, with half the roof gone, a mournful silhouette in the rising moonlight.

"Might as well get inside, for the night will be cold," Starella said, tying up Princess.

We crossed the threshold furtively. Inside was a huge hall with a gallery on three sides. It seemed to me that the place had been burnt down at some time and that this shell was all that remained.

"I don't like it," I said. "It's *wafodi*."

"It's a fine *filisin*," said Starella, meaning that it was a better mansion than either of us had ever been in. She spread the blanket on the broken boards and we cuddled down.

Starella was soon asleep but I lay rigid, hearing the little night sounds; a mouse running, a peewit calling, leaves rustling—these were all natural but there seemed to me to be an undertone of evil about the place, and it was vibrating.

About an hour later the moon went behind a cloud, and I heard a faint wailing sound begin, which grew into a moan and then a shriek. Starella woke at this and we both lay on our backs staring in petrified immobility at the gallery above. A figure, grey and wraithlike, floated across it and was gone. She looked for all the world like a nun. A few seconds later there was another shriek. This time it was Starella.

"*Shoovanis*," she screamed, "witches."

I followed her out under the starlit sky as the moon once more shone upon us, and I noticed it was full.

Princess, who had been dozing, was not as swift as we would have wished in her getaway, but before long we were back on a country *drom*, trotting briskly we knew not where, nor cared as long as it put distance between us and that awful place.

Towards dawn I could sense that Princess was tired and we stopped beneath some trees, only to realize that in our haste we had left the blanket behind. The grass was wet with dew and our sleep uncomfortable but at least it was uninterrupted.

The dawn chorus didn't even wake us and the sun was high in the sky by the time we opened our eyes (and perhaps in that time someone must have spotted us) to hear Princess snickering at the approach of someone or something. I looked across the meadow to where the road ran along behind the thick hedgerow.

A small shape appeared at the stile, a wild-looking, dishevelled and weary figure in the sunlight, limping slightly but coming on down the meadow with dogged determination, trailing with it a broken chain.

I squinted in the sunlight, then struggled to my feet and started to run.

"Rufus! Rufus! How did you follow, how did you get away? Rufus!" I flung my arms around him and he licked my face all over excitedly.

"Starella, look, here's Rufus."

"*Kooshti Duvel*," she said, rubbing her eyes. "Now what's he done? They'll all be after us now." But her voice held a tinge of 'don't care' in it and I knew, like me, she was tiring of our adventure.

"Come on Rufus, *kooshti juggal*. Look Starella, his paw do be bleedin'. And he's hungry, he's had no food." We took him to drink at the stream, talking all the time and wondering how he had managed to track us this far.

"He must have gone to the old woman's cottage and to the old house," said Starella, shuddering at the memory. We worked it out that he had probably followed the scent of Princess, but it all seemed a miracle.

The next problem was how to feed him. "He needs meat," I said. "And he's hungry, but if he goes chicken stealing he'll be shot by the *gorgios*."

"Aw, dinna you worry, *chal*," said Starella nonchalantly, "he'll hunt something for himself."

The problem was how to get on now that we had an injured dog with us. We let him rest under a tree and began to discuss whether he'd accept a ride on Princess's back.

But our council of campaign was unnecessary, for approaching us across the field from the road were two men, and this time one of them *was* a *plastramengro*. We didn't move; Rufus barked at first, Princess stopped cropping and silently all four of us watched as they came nearer. I think we knew the journey was over and that escape was impracticable.

Starella and I took each other's hands.

"You the two children from the Romany wedding down Thetford way?" asked the policeman. "The runaways?" We nodded. The other man, a farmer whose land this must be, had a shot-gun under his arm and I wondered if he'd ever imagined using it on us.

"Well," said the policeman, taking out his notebook, "I advise you to come along with me to the station, young people, for your parents do be making a frightful fuss about your disappearance together, and they'll be glad to know you're safe at last."

I thought not. They would be angry, I knew, and I realized what my punishment would be.

I was beaten, but both Starella and I were believed when we innocently told of our wish to get married, and that the journey was for this honourable purpose.

Starella's father at first almost went mad when he saw me, but I believe that he was convinced at last by my youthful frankness about the whole matter and that his daughter had come to no harm. In the end it was settled, first in anger, then with blows, then laughed off and forgotten.

One thing I can always say for the Romanies is that when dealing with one another they never hold a grudge.

Starella and I didn't meet again, even when she was married, and it was not to me. For by that time Hitler's war had begun and I had joined the RAF, and was training in Canada. My mother sent me photographs. I think she chose well. He was one of the best looking *roms* I've seen and certainly did not appear to have the air of a reluctant bridegroom, which I had had all those years before.

9

Show Business and Sloper Lusher

I was twelve and strong for my age when I rashly offered my services as organ pumper at the Congregational Church in Colchester. Somehow I was settling down nicely to a semi-permanent existence like the *gorgios*.

Every Sunday I pumped at each service and devoured volumes of Dickens given to me by Mr Christian Everett, the organist. Perhaps he regretted this generous gesture for I found *Barnaby Rudge* so fascinating that twice I forgot my purpose and the organ offended the ear of the choir and congregation with breathless groans and wheezy gasps.

"Here comes the pillar of our church," Mr Everett would say kindly as I arrived for duty. My pay was one shilling for services and two shillings and sixpence for weddings and funerals; I thought there was certainly something to be said for religion.

But this was no life for my father, nor, he considered, for his son—who seemed to be getting as set in his ways as a rate-payer! So one day it happened. A plumed and belled beast met my eyes on my return from church. "What's that?" I asked, only just recognizing one of the horses dolled up to the nines.

"It's for our new sideshow. We're going on the road. Come here and learn to stand on my shoulders. I'm going to ride the beast. Meet Heini and Algy—they're joining us." Two tattered figures saluted me, grinning. My father was going into show business and so, willy-nilly, was I.

The orchard in Lavenham had never witnessed such incredible goings-on. With the help of Heini and Algy—two wanderers who had surely seen better days—a draughty tent was rigged, but merely as an emergency measure should it rain.

These two layabouts proved to be zealots when it came to work connected with show business. Everything interested them, from setting up a rough stage to helping my mother make flour and water 'custard pies'.

In those days, when entertainment in the country was sparse and people were more innocent, my father's little show proved to be something of a success. Heini played the violin like an angel and could take his turn on the harmonica. Algy was agile and a good knock-about comic.

At dusk, one August Saturday, we put on our first show. Posters designed by my father's ever versatile hand had been up in the village for a week, advertising the great violinist 'Heineski' and the famous dramatic actor 'Algernon Byron', who had been tempted, at enormous expense, to join Gipsy Petulengro's players.

It was tuppence or sixpence to come and sit on a rickety bench for an hour. My mother sold the tickets at the orchard gate, tearing them in half with a flourish.

By keeping the stub of each ticket my father was able to keep toll of gate-crashers, though boys who climbed the ancient apple trees were hard to lay one's hands on. Nevertheless, when given the chance, my father laid his hands on and no messing.

I was filled with excitement as I watched the opening scenes. People had come from all the villages around, and the moving rows of faces, the fidgeting kids, the restless youngsters, the stolid farm-workers, the lined and cheerful-looking old people gave me my first taste of an audience.

Heini opened as a 'serious' violinist. Dressed in toeless boots, a bowler of brim only, checked trousers, a long swallow-tail coat and a very long scarf that caught under other people's feet almost strangling him, he murdered the classics in style.

I would double up laughing every night as I stood in the wings at the side of the stage, and so did the audience. It got them in a good mood for the rest of the show. Heini would play faster and faster, with frills and flourishes, hogging the audience, full of his own importance. The only thing that would put him in retreat was a battery of custard pies launched with indignant roars by my father and Algy, waiting to come on.

I always felt more anxious during my father's act, hoping that people would like him and that he should not fail. I would watch the kids' faces carefully through the bit of sacking at the side of the stage, aware that if it wasn't a good show and worth the money I'd get a bad time at school.

My father and Algy put on a song and dance act. My father played the accordion well, had a good baritone voice and looked very imposing in his gipsy costume. Algy danced; some nights it was a Dutch clog dance and on others a tap routine, but most popular was the mock ballet routine when he wore tights which, on his skinny legs, fell in wrinkles and looked anything but tight and in great danger of descending during the performance.

The script for the cross-talk act was not impressive but it seemed hilarious to me.

My father as a judge: "Tell me, my man, have you ever been up before me?"

Heini as a villain: "I don't know. What time do you get up?"

Even religion was treated lightly. One was the story of a travelling circus performer who went to a Catholic priest for confession one quiet day in a new village, when only two ladies were in the church. The circus tumbler was feeling depressed.

"Father," he said, "I feel I'm no use in the world, I get no satisfaction from my work."

"That is nothing to worry about, my boy. But I'm not sure what work you do. Go down the aisle and show me; I'll watch from here." So the tumbler did three back somersaults down the aisle.

"Mother of God," cried one of the old ladies, rising from her pew. "If that's the penance Father's handing out today, I'm off."

The finale was preceded by my ride round the orchard on one of the horses. I had learned to stand on his back; this was not in itself difficult, but avoiding the low branches of the apple trees demanded a fair amount of skill and several times I was left swinging from a branch.

Finale time included a sing-song with the audience, which they thoroughly enjoyed, to the music of my father's accordion.

We began to move on to other Suffolk villages and thence into Norfolk. It was in one of the sleepy Norfolk villages that my father met up with Sloper Lusher. Sloper was a farm labourer, abnormally tall and well known locally for his slow speech and sloping, loping walk.

By now we were in the big-time and able to book village halls with a real stage and curtains. But my father wanted the extra money of a side-show. "How'd you like to make some easy money, Sloper boy?" asked my father one night in the pub, his eyes twinkling, and with a sly pull at his moustache.

"Thar's arl righ'with me, boy. But how's I gonna do thar?" answered Sloper.

My father outlined his scheme.

The village blacksmith was commissioned to make a cage. Several nights later Sloper, drawn by the exciting prospect of having his name in lights, turned up for rehearsal and make-up.

Blacked up, curtain rings dangling from his ears, topped by a curly black wig and dressed only in a sheepskin, Sloper climbed into the cage and proceeded to make faces through the bars. He was thrown food by my father, whose fairground patter went like this: "Roll up, roll up, ladies and gentlemen. Come and see the wild man of Borneo, discovered and captured by me and Professor Copsy, the well-known explorer, and brought back to this country at enormous expense."

It was tuppence to see him and perhaps some customers considered that to be an enormous expense, too, but the joke was well taken.

"Thar be ol' Sloper, thar be," some would mutter, but others from outlying villages were more easily taken in. In any case, Sloper enjoyed it if no one else did and welcomed the opportunity to make his name as an actor, even though he was under oath not to utter a word in his broad Norfolk voice, but roar as a wild man should.

In his act Sloper was supposed to walk on a hot iron. The rod was not really very hot and Sloper's feet were waxed with a special ointment my father had made up so that for the split second involved he felt nothing.

As he became accustomed to making himself up Sloper took to changing at home and riding from his mother's cottage on a bicycle in costume. It was a weird sight, and one calculated to enrage my father, who felt potential customers were getting a free look.

One night Sloper, who had been obliged to work overtime on the farm, arrived late. He carefully locked himself in the cage, but forgot to wax his feet.

"Oh Christ!" he shouted as his toe touched the iron.

"The only two words of English he knows, ladies and gentlemen," called my father with brilliant alacrity. "Taught to him by the missionaries."

With the onset of winter the show folded. Algy left the cast, having fallen in love, married and become a butler in a gentle-man's country house. Although he was in many senses a gentleman himself, sensitive and good-looking, I could not imagine how he had got the job and pictured him landing custard pies in his master's face at the dinner table.

Heini, too, faded into the mists of the unknown. My father had discovered him, a true busker, ragged but happy, walking along the gutter. I often wonder if he returned there, happy as ever.

10

Travellers All

As I have said, my father was a travellin' man, always restless, never content to be in one place for more than a few months at the most, always itching to be off somewhere new or familiar.

He was aware of his 'superiority' as a Romany, yet had great respect for other travellers, knights of the road, and one of his favourite pastimes was to describe and catalogue their virtues and faults for me or anyone who would listen.

"*Gorgios* have the idea that anyone they meet on the road is a gipsy," he used to begin, "this is not so." He felt strongly the injustice to the true Romanies who were very proud and romantic people with a code of behaviour, a tribal solidity, a conscience and indeed a group charisma. We were to him the kings of the *drom*.

The people he allowed himself to despise he called *moochers*; these were the *gorgio* tramps, the tattered dishevelled dropouts who wandered about without background or skills. They could not snare a rabbit or a hare, or catch a fish and barely knew how to keep a fire going, let alone cook on it!

They'd beg at the door for their bread, hoping their sorry appearance would bring extras in the form of hot tea with milk and sugar. We thought *moochers* were lazy and dirty scroungers who may have come down in the world through 'drink or stupidity', as Xavier was wont to sneer.

He had a little more respect for the half-breed Romany

tramps called *didikais* who worked for their living. Many of them were hardly half-bred for all that, because little or no gipsy blood had been allowed into this country over the last fifty years and there is hardly any Romany blood left in them. They wander around and copy the Romany lore by using signs as a language to tell others where good-hearted people live. In spite of this Xavier did not disapprove. The great virtue of these people, according to him, was that they did not beg.

There were many trades among them. For instance, the *chiv barrer* or knife and scissor-grinder, was a familiar sight of my childhood. His 'wheels' were mostly made by himself from a piece of circular wood and covered with a piece of leather which he dressed by covering them with glue and rolling them in powdered emery.

During the course of a week the *chiv barrer* would call at doors collecting a dozen or more pairs of 'snips' which he would take away and grind, then redeliver them. For this he charged a few pence, but it was usually enough to pay his lodging or *kip* for the night.

Another *didikai* worker was the *cane-fakir*, who mended cane-seated chairs.

The *mush-fakirs* who mended or made umbrellas were aristocrats of skill. The steel-framed umbrella finally did away with the trade, but before the advent of its mass production, the umbrella (or pikey) used widely over the countryside was of whalebone. Many a farmer owned a *pikey-mush*, six feet across, for use when out in his gig; and wonderful they looked too.

The *taso-fakir*, or china-mender, has also inherited his skills from the Romanies. A drill and rivets are used to piece the shattered bits together, however many there might be, and sometimes the result looked better than new! My Uncle Rudy, who was my father's younger brother, was a *taso-fakir*, and once mended a Ming vase that had been broken in a hundred pieces—or so Xavier liked to tell. Unhappily I never met him because he died when quite young, having been set on at a fair by a group of *gorgios*.

But my father's deepest disdain was for the *shallow-runner*, a tramp who lived deliberately in tatters in order to excite pity in the middle-class housewives who opened their doors to him. Many a time he'd come away with a beautiful suit of clothes, only slightly frayed at the edges, and would sell it for profit, still wearing his rags and tatters. These as often as not found their way to the *tog-fencer*, a market worker who sold clothes.

Some of the descriptions shouted from the stall of one of my father's favourite characters, a real *tog-fencer* of Colchester market, were highly original. If you were lucky you could easily buy the 'Hearl of Spencer's hold dress-suit'. Or perhaps you cared to take on 'Lord 'Umphries' larvely lounge suit for 'arf a dollar'. Big Bill was cockney to his back teeth, and never let on where his clothes came from; they may very well have dropped off the back of a lorry, but my father's bet was that he got them mostly from the *shallow-runners*.

My father's trading practices often led him to the 'Ditch' for 'swag'. In those days the Houndsditch Warehouse in East London was not the palace it is today. It consisted of a few little shops. A kindly old Jew stood in the doorway of one greeting my father with great joy and rubbing of hands. "Now, vot is it zat you vont today? Have you done good business zis month? Good, good, vot can I show you?"

Then Xavier would order four dozen boxes of cotton thread on reels (in assorted colours), and leather bootlaces (a penny for two laces when he sold them to country folk). "Ayee, you take many pairs of bootlaces today," the old Jew would remark, fussing around, afraid to allow one second of silence to pass as if it were a bad omen. *Maison Bleue* was another shop we frequented together. It was owned by a French Jew of refinement who was slightly more choosy about his stock: jewels, watches, clocks, and teaspoons.

Back home, Xavier the middle-man would sell most of his stock to two other pedlars who could not afford to lay out the necessary capital of fifty pounds or so for large orders, but would take two or three cotton reels at a time, a couple of dozen pairs of bootlaces, some needles, six Old Moore's Almanacs, skeins of wool and so on.

It may be the time to say here that Old Moore's Almanac was a familiar of my childhood with Xavier. I learnt a great deal of my astrology from it because it gave all the various planet movements during the year.

Sent by my father on a sales mission, I'd walk the lanes of Suffolk on my way to village doors, reading it avidly before the customers could lay their hands on its precious pages. My commission from Xavier was one halfpenny a copy.

A cheerful and fairly confident spieler, like all good Sagittarians, I footslogged my way round the villages, devouring the printed words like sweets. After all, a salesman, I reasoned, should know what he was selling—and I certainly did! I learned from Old Moore the transits of the planets, the signs of the zodiac, the waxing and waning of the moon, and their various portents.

The gloominess of the predictions had me in thrall. The illustrations told all. A Chinaman with a sinister dagger dripping blood—trouble in China; Uncle Sam and John Bull shaking hands across the sea—good news for the allies; Old Father Time, the reaper—bad news; tall smoking chimneys and grim flat-capped men walking in their shadow (presumably, for only the heads were shown)—'industrial unrest'.

A lot of it made my hair stand on end, but it was better than reading Billy Bunter.

One old girl who was a regular customer couldn't read a word of it, yet she wanted to know everything that was predicted. So she would regularly invite me in for a glass of milk and some of her home-made saffron buns, whenever I was passing; and I, the Romany scholar, would read to her of trouble and disputes, of assassinations and celebrations and wars and *ententes cordiales* (which I am sure she believed to be some kind of summer drink and, indeed, who was I to enlighten her?) while she nodded and smiled or looked suitably solemn.

As the price of the Almanac was only threepence and I spent nearly an hour reading the contents of the same tattered copy on each monthly visit, I do not think my father would have considered my sales methods very efficient in that case, but I felt that it was a service I could not refuse the old lady, and I went on my way glowing with virtue.

It may have been my mother's influence which made me so much less of an extrovert than Xavier, or perhaps it was in my genes to be so, for I found when I was travelling with him in public that he could cause me enormous embarrassment once I had reached the age of awareness that is called puberty.

Travelling on trains was especially painful for me because Xavier was almost certain to get into an argument. We often travelled by this method to London, buying a return ticket and boarding at Colchester Grand Central Station, so to speak. (The other was St Botolph's, or, as pronounced by the locals, 'Bottles'.)

There would always be some fairly respectable watch-chain type gentlemen in the compartment. There was no corridor in those days, nor long open carriages, and we were forced to sit in rows of six facing each other, imprisoned in a narrow box-like compartment which stretched from side to side.

Of course, everyone would stare when Xavier got into the carriage sporting his broad-brimmed black Stetson, his huge hoop ear-rings, and his 'swag' bags, empty, as if belonging to some hopeful burglar. There would be a rustling of *The Times* or the *Morning Post* and heads would disappear behind these barriers after the first long stare was over. Xavier would then read out aloud to me imaginary and highly improbable bits purported to be from the backs of these papers, much to the owners' discomfiture and my intense embarrassment: "On the trail of the bloodstained kipper! Detective Sergeant Pokenose, in his statement today, said that the police were now investigating a very important point—who put the pepper in the cat's milk?"

I was acutely embarrassed, knowing he was only doing it to provoke animosity. Slimy little toady that I was, I somehow felt ingratiating towards these stuffed shifts at that age, although I later grew out of it.

Then would come the crisis. Xavier would light up one of his noxious herb cigarettes and take deep, contented pulls. Soon a man next to the window would open it. Xavier, after suffering for a few minutes the icy blasts, would get up and shut it. (He may have been a gipsy, but he believed that when you were outside you were outside, and when you were inside, well, that was another thing entirely and it was madness to open a window and let out expensively heated air, and to let in cold air in its place.)

A moment or two would pass, and down would come the window, the culprit disappearing behind his paper once the deed was done. That did it. Bang! Up flew the window like a yo-yo.

"If you're so bloody hot," said Xavier rudely to the indignant and dumbfounded passenger, "get out and sit on the bloody roof." End of contest.

Once at Liverpool Street Station it was a short walk to the 'Ditch', and we would set off and do our business there in no time; then it was time to return to the station and make for home.

Sometimes, when we lived in Norfolk, we used to take Sloper along on these excursions to the great metropolis. He loved the idea of visiting 'Lunnon'. All he ever saw, alas, was Liverpool Street, and that had to suffice, for he was too scared to put his nose outside once he caught a glimpse of the teeming streets, and used to await our return decorously sitting on a station bench watching the crowds go by.

He told some dreadful lies on his return and got a fine reputation as an adventurer among country folk, who were never told the truth of the matter by my father or me. In actual fact Sloper was useful to us, for we could leave the newly-acquired 'swag' with him once we returned to the station, and set off for Lyons to indulge ourselves in their delicious tea, served in a plated pot, and some Chelsea buns with butter. This for me was the high spot and so I welcomed Sloper's presence, for without him the feast would have been impossible. After the feast came the *rechnung* as the Germans say, and this was the enormous sum of fivepence each.

One of the highlights of the travellin' man's year was Derby Day, a day I looked forward to all year round. We'd take the vardo on a five-day journey, parking on the Epsom Downs by night before the meeting and greeting once again the different tribes of Romanies—the Boswells, the Lovells, the Greys, the Smiths, the Lloyds—who we searched out among the riff-raff who were also parked there.

Xavier gave tips on horses for money, and he was very often right, so he was considered good value. He could sense a horse was a winner just by looking at it, and I must confess that although I never bet and never now go to the racecourse, I have inherited this gift—something about the nostrils, the set of the mane, the hock, the withers, the pace of the horse, tells me what I want to know, and it was so for my father, too.

I cannot place bets from a distance, or by studying form. I have to see the horse.

So, Xavier's dealings at the Derby were honest. But there were some there who were rogues and he pointed them out to me.

"See, Lion, how they trick. Look at this *moosh* here; he's the three-cards trickster." They are still about today. If ever you have been asked to 'find the lady' in Oxford Street, you'll know how hopeless a gamble it is for the innocent bystander.

One trick that fascinated me was the half-crown trick. The trickster makes play with a few half-crowns, which he throws in the air with one hand and then into a purse held in his other hand. Clinking away, the money falls straight into his hollowed palm underneath the open purse. Inside the purse are pennies. Now the man turns to you for the crunch.

"Come on mister, come on lady, what say you buy this purse for just one half-crown. Just one half-crown in exchange for half a dozen. Isn't that a bargain?" If you were fool enough you'd fall for it, and you'd get a bag of pennies. But you didn't complain or tell the police, because you felt such a fool.

My father was careful to point out to me that he didn't approve of such things and that the only honest way to behave was to offer goods or services for money. His one exception in the year was Derby Day when he gave out his tips—but these were genuine and in good faith, too.

Travellin' with my father was always an adventure. I learned so much from him when we did *coor the drom* together, for he was generous in his sharing of knowledge and he made all our journeys so entertaining.

I am one of those who believes that it is better to travel than to arrive. At least, that is what I thought as a child; and I was probably right.

It always will be the *boro-drom*, the highway, that calls me . . .

11

Silly Suffolk

Suffolk has always been my favourite county. Early travels with Xavier took me often to the North, land of giant factory chimneys belching acrid smoke like old men with their pipes; to Buckinghamshire and Surrey, where I saw gorse and firs and butterflies; to Bristol and the West where the land rolls and the rain clouds pile in from the Atlantic or the Irish Sea; and to Wales where the view from one valley to another is a wonder as you *coor the drom*. But it was to Suffolk that we returned time and time again, and there it was we finally settled.

Suffolk is a place for smiles, slow, paced by country rhythms; listening, waiting, the countryside unrolls gently under changing skies. Suffolk with its Constable trees and languid streams and soft patois. Voices in that fair county seem to murmur with an underlying burble of a laugh, deep chuckles seem to burst forth with the pronouncement of each syllable.

It's those voices I miss most when I'm away. The Suffolkese that is a homely sound, and has changed little since the day I first heard it.

"Whoi, missus, yar hat's all of a-huh."

'A-huh' means lop-sided. There are many words not found in the Oxford English Dictionary, for instance 'arternune'. One neighbour to another as an elderly lady passes by: "Oi do reckon she's gittin' into the arternune!" (i.e. getting on a bit.)

'Silly' means something entirely different to the definition given in the OED. "You don't want to hang them pitchers too silly high." In this case it means excessively, or very. 'Sarnick' means to loiter, as I soon learned. "Whoi, boy," said one old Suffolk man to me, taking his pipe out of his mouth with a chuckle, "how you dew go a' sarnickin' along." (I was' dawdling to school.)

'Charley' is a toad, 'cow mumble' is cow parsley, and a 'diddle' is a duck. To 'ding' is to throw, hurl or hit. For instance: "Oi give him a ding about the lug-hole." ('Give' used here as past tense.) In Suffolk 'don't' is used like do, so: "Do you hurry up or don't you'll miss the train."

And you still hear, "Gimme the paper. I just want to look at the gays." (Give me the paper, I just want to look at the pictures.)

As for 'owd', well you can't understand Suffolkese unless you know that word. "My little owd dog, my little owd horse." Normally it doesn't mean old except in an affectionate way. Have you heard of a 'King Harry'? It's a kingfisher. And if I told you I wanted to 'kiddle' you, it means I want to embrace you.

Finally, they don't mind calling a spade a spade in Suffolk—upside-down is 'arse-uppards'. And don't confuse the word 'bor' with boy, which is also used, but in a different sense. 'Bor' means neighbour, and is derived from Old English and the Low German 'bur' for countryman. The plural is the word 'togither'. "Oi don't know about you togither, but oi'm a'gooin' hoom."

So as the Romanies say, "*Kooshti bok, kooshti sante, kooshti divvas* . . ." Good luck, good health and good day to you all . . . As a small child I knew two languages, Suffolkese and Romany, and could talk in either with ease.

As I said, Suffolk is my home. Mind you, I am not too

particular about the border line between Suffolk and Essex, so if at times I wander you'll have to forgive me.

One of East Anglia's greatest children, apart from Nelson and Cromwell, was John Constable, and the village he confessed he loved best was East Bergholt, where he met and married his wife. He wrote: "I love every stile and stump and lane in the village; as long as I am able to hold a brush I shall never cease to paint them." Luckily for us, he kept to his word.

One of the village's most famous recent inhabitants was Randolph Churchill, who lived near the old church in a fine Georgian house, of which there are several in the village. The church itself is unusual in that it has an unfinished broken tower and the bells are housed in a wooden sixteenth-century house next door.

My father told me the legend. It is said that every time the builders built up the tower during the day the Devil came and destroyed their work at night, but I was later told by a less imaginative and more erudite gentleman that Wolsey—an Ipswich man—was financing the tower and when he came to no good the tower was abandoned.

My favourite town of course is Lavenham, used much nowadays for films and television serials to portray the typical medieval town. It is crowded with tourists in the summer, yet it keeps its character and is not so very different from the days when I wandered its streets as a boy.

In the Middle Ages there was a prospering woollen industry around Lavenham. The mill-owners built themselves large houses with unusually high ceilings to accommodate the looms.

Xavier used to say that Lavenham was the first village in England to have a sugar factory and that he distinctly remembered, when he was young, speaking to the French engineers who were setting it up. It was burnt down in 1905 and later rebuilt and converted into a store for horse hair fabric and coconut matting, for in the late eighteen hundreds and even into this century, Lavenham was famed as a horse hair weaving centre. The fabric was used for covering couches and seats of railway carriages and for stiffening the shoulders of suits and jackets.

Lavenham has a unique water supply. It flows through a pipe which runs through the cottages, and at the gable end of one cottage is the spout from which water runs continually day and night. They call it Water Street.

Kersey and Lindsey, the nearest villages, I knew well. I used to wander their tree-lined streets, often knocking on doors in order to tout the wares my father had loaded on me for the day. I always met with kindness.

At Polstead I was aware of a sinister feeling, for if you've ever heard of a melodrama called 'Murder in the Red Barn', you can be sure the story is not fiction but fact. It actually happened in Polstead, the village which stands so prettily in a valley by the banks of the River Box.

Near the village church could be found one of the largest trees in the country. Folk called it the Gospel Oak. It was thirty-two feet around the trunk five feet from the ground.

But back to our story and its villain. William Corder, a local farmer, courted and won a beautiful villager called Maria Marten, but when trouble came he brutally murdered her with a spade and buried her in the 'Red Barn'. Her stepmother had for three nights in succession a vivid dream which was prophetic and eventually led to the discovery of the place of burial. William Corder was later traced at Brentford where he had married a rich woman; he was brought back to be sentenced and hanged in 1828 at Bury St Edmunds, before ten thousand watchers! His skeleton is in Suffolk General Hospital.

The Red Barn is no more, but Maria Marten's thatched cottage exists to this day, and charabancs full of morbid-minded trippers travel to see it each summer. Passing it as a *chal*, I couldn't stop a slight shiver running up and down my body.

There are so many beautiful villages to be found in Suffolk and, unfortunately, today, the tourist knows them too. But if you want to find the real Suffolk, hidden away, secret and to itself, then take my advice and go north of Woodbridge to villages like Dallinghoo, Cretingham, Kettleburgh and Hoo. There are fine little churches and Tudor farmhouses and, provided you like farming land, you'll not be disappointed.

Much of my early life was centred on Sudbury, that most ancient of the 'wool towns'. It was here that Gainsborough was born in 1727, the youngest of nine children of a non-conformist woollen crêpe-maker. There's a statue of him on Sudbury Market Hill. Sudbury was once a flourishing port on the River Stour; John Constable painted its barges and I can remember the last of them before 1930 being sent to Dedham.

The Suffolk of my childhood was indeed a magic land with its own language. There were 'paigles' (cowslips) in the meadows, and 'polliwogs' (tadpoles) in the ponds, 'horpies' (lapwings) on the fields, and 'hoss needles' (dragon-flies) down by the streams. The flash of the white scut of a 'botsy' (rabbit) as you came round the hedge into a field was a familiar sight. At night the 'barley bird' (nightingale) sang and 'charley', the toad, eyed you lazily from the mud. It was a land where 'cow mumble' (cow parsley) grew in snowy drifts.

And with spring came the 'goslins', the willow-catkins; the dawn chorus began at four and as the sun rose you could, if you were a child, 'sarnick' (dawdle) along listening to the 'pudden-e-poke' (long-tailed tit). But for most it was still a hard time. His labour was all man could sell in the country-side of those days as had been the case for centuries, and the labour was still hard when I was a boy, with very little mechanization, apart from the odd chaff-cutter!

Even so, there were plenty of women who enjoyed a good

'sarnick' and 'mardle' (gossip) with my mother and even if you only had bread and pull-it to eat, the summer days would make you forget the long, hard, cold, wet winters when from the bare trees the 'dun billys' (crows) cawed with gruesome warning, for in the spring they would think nothing of picking out a lamb's eye a few moments after birth.

Wherever I wandered, Suffolk remained in the back of my mind like a magic lantern slide, a reminder that she was waiting, to hold me in familiar arms again like a comforting mother.

Essex, her neighbour, was my friend too, and in later years my mother and father, so long together, were to split up, for he bought her a little house in Colchester, which she loved and never stopped cleaning and shining while he was off round the country with his band of gipsy players.

What is Colchester famous for? Roses, oysters and as the oldest Roman settlement in the country. In Childwell Alley there was a spring where those suffering from poor eyesight could bathe their eyes and be healed, a practice going back to Roman days.

In Layer-de-la-Haye I stalked many a butterfly in the woods where there grew ferns and bluebells, and where the fences were entwined with honeysuckle. Today all is cut down and the great A12 highway curves out of London towards Colchester bringing the delights of the countryside nearer, yet destroying so much in its wake, too.

The great decline in the number of butterflies, for instance, mainly due to modern farming methods and re-afforestation, is a painful thing to think about today. One species in particular, the Large Blue, is almost extinct and probably cannot be saved.

Anyeta, besides her other talents, was something of a naturalist and knew many butterflies on sight. The Essex Skipper, the Grizzled Skipper, the Brimstone, the Cabbage White, the Camberwell Beauty, the Duke of Burgundy

Fritillary, the Meadow Brown, the Peacock, and many more.

Long before modern researchers found out about the Large Blue and its life-cycle, Anyeta would tell me of its strange life; how it hatched from an egg laid in the bell of the blossom of wild thyme, how it fed on the thyme blossoms and shed its skin once, twice; then a honey-gland appeared and after the third shedding of its skin the caterpillar, fat with food, fell to the ground and wandered away in search of an ant, which would milk it of its honey then carry it off to the nest, where it slept the winter with strange bedfellows—the ant larvae.

Anyeta's story was proved to be true by researchers, whose research shows that with the coming of spring the caterpillar becomes a chrysalis, remains in a coma for three weeks, then a butterfly is born which, still less than a glorious creature, somehow finds its way along the halls and galleries of its hosts' castle to the air above. After drying its wings it flies away, mates, lays eggs, and dies within fifteen days.

If you're in search of beauty, you'll find it in Essex in the creeks of those villages between Tollesbury and West Mersea. On the mud flats as the tide creeps in over the salt flats you'll see ducks, curlew, widgeon and bar geese—or they were there when I was young. In Suffolk they call a sprat a 'sparling'. In Essex in the little town of Brightlingsea they used to harvest millions of sprats from the sea, and many were exported. An average of seventeen hundred bushels a day would leave for Ostend in the industry's heyday, and the biggest catch by one ship, the *Marion*, was five hundred bushels!

When I was young Brightlingsea had its 'Sprat Queen', Mrs Gould. She was the great exporter behind the industry, a lively lady who never let anything go to waste. The sprats that were caught too late for market or despatch overseas that day, she bought from the fishermen and sent on lorries to distant farms to be used as manure.

In Tiptree, too, was a very famous Essex industry, for it

was there that the celebrated family firm of jam-makers began and still thrives.

One of my father's many jobs as a young man was to photograph the fruit in full ripe glory for advertisement brochures. He told me he became so good at this that Tiptree sent him abroad with the vardo and his wife to photograph the orange orchards near Seville from where they imported the best fruit to make their famous marmalade. The journey took a whole year.

He always told me that I was born in Spain, a fact I was too young to confirm, for my first memories are certainly of that peaceful Lavenham orchard with its apple trees and not of any stronger sun or brighter fruit!

When I asked how we came back into England and whether I had to have a passport, he told me I was smuggled in. So perhaps I am one of the first illegal immigrants. I hope HM Government will allow me to stay after all this time.

12

Legends of the Gipsies

As a child I often experienced pre-vision. I would say to Xavier: "Round the next corner there will be a large house with wistaria and a dovecot. In the garden there is a man working."

Sure enough it was so. As our caravan rounded the bend the scene I had described would meet our eyes, yet I had never been that way before. It was this gift that persuaded my father that I had inherited some of the psychic skill of my grandmother.

Most of my visions were not earth-shattering and only concerned my immediate surroundings. But there was one, once in my life, which seemed to me to be of greater significance, and I have never been able to forget it.

I was at the time an RAF rear-gunner stationed at St Eval, Cornwall, on 'ops' with Coastal Command. One beautiful spring morning I had decided, after a night on patrol duty, to walk the few miles to St Columb to send a parcel to my mother from the post office there. I had had no sleep, but did not want to waste the perfect day.

The yellow-hammers were busy in the hedgerows, chirping their claim to territory; celandine and stitchwort glowed among the grassy verges; in the distance a skylark rose on a crest of clear, warbling notes.

There were no aircraft about and I felt at peace. My footsteps made the only sound on the narrow road. I had walked about a mile when I saw a tall figure coming towards me. He held a staff in his hand, his feet were shod in sandals, a brown robe was loosely belted. As we drew closer I noticed that his gaze was direct, his face thin, with a brown beard, his hair long. There was a monastery some miles away and I took him to be a friar.

We passed close and I greeted him in country fashion: "Good morning." His only reply was a smile as radiant as sunshine, a smile from his eyes.

A few seconds later I turned to have another look, but he had gone. I knew that he could not have disappeared through the thick and tangled hedges, there were no ditches, no bend for several hundred yards and there had not been a farm gate for a quarter of a mile. Yet he was no longer in sight. I did not feel disturbed by the experience, but elated. I have told no one of it until now and I remember it without any sense of spookiness, merely with pleasure.

Anyeta's psychic gifts were legend in our tribe. She once predicted for my father that he would speak to millions without ever seeing their faces. Since this was before the advent of radio it was very strange that she should so accurately predict his BBC broadcasts with Freddie Grisewood in the 'thirties.

Superstition and belief in the supernatural is part of Romany living and many weird ghost tales were told round the *yag* at night, passed on by word of mouth from generation to generation.

The most gripping and beautiful tale of all was the story of St Sara, the first Romany Christian, and this was my favourite when I was a boy.

Sara was a gipsy chieftain in France who had a vision which converted her to Christianity—for the vision, according to my grandmother, was prophetic, and what she saw came to pass.

She saw three saints who were in a boat which had struck rough weather, and was about to capsize at the mouth of the

River Rhône. She realized that they were calling for her help.

Sara set out for the spot she had seen in her dream and, lo and behold, there were the three saints, adrift in a storm not far from the river's mouth, but unable to make it to shore. Then Sara threw her cloak on the waves and stepping upon it, moved over the sea towards them. She reached them just as their boat sank, and they climbed upon the 'raft' which was Sara's cloak, and, using the oars from the boat, rowed back to shore.

Sara was baptized and became a maidservant of the three saints, and thereafter converted all her tribe to Christianity. And the three saints were Mary Jacoby, Mary Magdalene and Mary Salome who had all been present at the Cross some hundreds of years before.

The name given by the gipsies to Sara, when in 1496 they chose her as their saint, was *'la Kali'* the black woman, also meaning 'the gipsy woman'.

It was the established Catholic Church itself which initially established the famous pilgrimage of the 24th and 25th of May, after a successful investigation by King René during which the remains of the three saints were excavated from beneath the primitive little church of Notre Dame de Ratis (later Of The Three Marys). Subsequently a bronze chest was found in which lay the bones of Sara, and in 1438 those gipsies who were in Arles at that time, joined the pilgrimage, but as I have said, it was not until later in 1496 that they adopted Sara as their saint.

The pilgrimage is a two-day renewal of their faith by the Romany tribes, many of whom travel hundreds of miles to take part. On the night of the 24th the little crypt below the church is full of gipsies who keep vigil there, praying or sleeping or gazing. They do not practise any rites beyond two on their arrival. As they enter they hang garments on the statue of their saint, which is painted black, and they touch the saint with other objects representing their sick or dying at home—a photograph or some small possession of the affected person.

The second part of the pilgrimage is a journey to the sea and a symbolic total immersion. Anyeta had taken part in this pilgrimage and would describe it to me, the colour, the intensity of feeling, the joy and the silence alternating. Whenever she was silent and brooding I would wonder if she was remembering once again her pilgrimage to the gipsy saint all those years ago, and I would long to be able to take part myself.

The Roman Catholic faith was strong in a large number of Romany tribes over the centuries, but with the coming of the Reformation many turned to Protestantism. My parents were seldom in church, but they were in their way deeply religious and extremely moral. Many Romanies in years gone by enjoyed going to the country churches and made a big occasion of Sunday worship by putting on their best *togs*, as you may see from this passage from George Borrow's book *The Romany Rye*, concerning my namesakes of the nineteenth century.

"Mr Petulengro was dressed in Roman fashion, with a somewhat smartly cut sporting coat, the buttons of which were half-crowns, and a waistcoat scarlet and black, the buttons of which were spaded half-guineas; his breeches were of a stuff half-velveteen, half-corduroy, the cords exceeding broad. He had leggings of buff cloth, furred at the bottom, and upon his feet were high-lows. Under his left arm was a long black whalebone riding whip, with a red lash, and immense silver knob. Upon his head was a hat with a high peak, somewhat of the kind that the Spanish call *calanes*, so much in favour with the *bravos* of Seville and Madrid. Now when I have added that Mr Petulengro had on a very fine white holland shirt, I think I have described his array. Mrs Petulengro . . . was also arrayed very much

in the Roman fashion. Her hair, which was exceedingly
black and lustrous, fell in braids on either side of her head.
In her ears were rings with long drops of gold. Round her
neck was a string of what seemed very much like large
pearls, somewhat tarnished, however, and apparently of
considerable antiquity."

Such splendour. My parents rarely dressed so for church,
but they always put on their best.

Legend and lucky charms are vital to Romany philosophy
and no gipsy feels this to be a contradiction to the Christian
religion. In his philosophy they live side by side. Young
Romany *chis* and *chals* were romantic in their outlook on love,
passionate but not promiscuous, and the *chis* were always
searching for signs of love or messages about their future
lover.

To find a swan's feather floating on a stream was a
wonderful omen of eager love reciprocated.

Then there is the charm of the Romany bag—a draw-string
shammy bag filled with several charms: the foot of a rabbit, a
piece of the herb rosemary, some rue, three small stones, four
different sorts of straw, some wheat, oats, barley, rye, all
placed in a bag which was tightly closed and placed under the
pillow on a special date of the girl's choosing, so that she
should dream of her lover and see his face.

Another superstition was to find a stone with a hole in it,
thread a bootlace through this and tie it; then, taking three
circular swings, fling the stone up to a tree branch and see if it
hung there or fell to the ground. If it hung there dangling from
a branch, then the girl would be married in a few months'
time, but if the stone fell to the ground she would not be
married for many moons.

The nutmeg spell was also popular. A nutmeg is used for a
charm and cut into four equal pieces. One part is buried in
the ground, one in water, one in the ashes of a fire, and the

last part is boiled and the liquid drunk. Then the nutmeg piece was taken from the water and placed under the *juval*'s pillow, whereupon she had sweet dreams knowing that no one would ever take her lover from her!

When Anyeta was part of the tribe in Romania, many a young *chal*, desperately in love with some beautiful *chi* would come to her for the herb potion that will make his love accept his suit.

Anyeta often used the method whereby the boy himself must go to the bank of the river and pick a certain leaf, then, pricking his own wrist and smearing the leaf with his blood, he must throw the leaf into the river, saying his own name and the name of his true love.

Another Romany charm that the gipsy passed to the *gorgios* eventually—and this became mostly the mark of the sailor—was tattooing. At first, hundreds of years ago, it was a mainly magical practice against the evil eye. Later, tattooing became purely adornment, mainly on the cheeks and chin, never on the body, and the designs were always abstract—no 'I love mother' or an erotic mermaid, this would have been deemed madness and the essence of bad taste.

Martin Block has described this art, which was widely practised in Persia, especially by the women of the tribe.

"Three or nine sharp needles, made by the Gipsies themselves, are tied together in a cluster, but not before first having had the appropriate formula spoken over them; nothing relating to magic is ever done in silence. Then the woman practitioner takes the set of needles, presses the points into the patient's cheek, and begins her work as '*pointilliste*' at the chosen place, until the blood spurts. She then plunges the needle into a liquid prepared beforehand; and continues the operation. The subject does not allow the slightest grimace to betray the pain, which is really torture. It is remarkable that the wound does not cause inflammation. It seems that the liquid used prevents this. Even in ancient times the evil eye was warded off with a mixture of charcoal soot, mineral oil, child's urine and plum alcohol. German superstition also attributed this practice to witches; in any case the mixture is a natural disinfectant . . ."

There is no doubt that if Anyeta had lived in fifteenth-century England she might have been burnt as a witch. With her curative and psychic powers she was indeed a magical person. In medieval Europe with its domination by a narrow-visioned Church anybody with as much pagan vitality and joyful energy as the gipsies was highly suspect to a population which was more or less rooted to the spot, either by dint of serfdom or other types of poverty and wretchedness which prevented their leaving the place of their birth.

A stranger with a swarthy face and rings in his ears was a very suspicious character and not to be trusted. These horse dealers, mountebanks, performers, fortune-tellers and smiths, were not to be tolerated in that society, for there was a lot of joy about them. Such devilish happiness smacked of the devil, and was not in line with the thinking of a formal and dogma-dominated religion, such as Christianity under the Popes had then become.

> "Wizards, witches and diviners
> Knaves, horse-copers,
> Saracens, Jews, convicted thieves,
> Debauchees, rakes and ribalds . . ."

So said the poet Deschamps, and the Saracens of that knavish lot were most certainly the gipsies.

There are many legends surrounding the gipsies, and one of the best known is the story giving the explanation for the saying that the Romanies may steal every seven years.

It is said that while the procession of Our Lord to Calvary

was resting for a while by the roadside, an old gipsy woman came upon the crowd and asked what was happening. When she was told, and saw the look of anguish on Our Lord's face, she felt great sorrow and wondered to herself how best to stop the Crucifixion taking place.

She decided that the best way was to steal the nails. She stole one and threw it away, but at the next attempt she was caught and thrashed by the Roman soldiers.

The old gipsy begged to be given mercy and said, "I haven't stolen anything for seven years."

On hearing this, one of the disciples standing near her said: "You are blessed now. The Saviour allows you to steal once every seven years from now onward." Anyeta used to say that was why only three nails were used on the Cross and the feet of Jesus were nailed together.

Anyeta was, herself, very religious, and rarely set about making one of her herbal cures without asking for a little help from the *Kooshti Duvel*. She wished for and received a Christian burial. But she was, being Romany, superstitious as well, and saw no reason why the two should not go hand-in-hand. She was a great one for spinning yarns and passing on the legends of Romany lore, and when I was very small I was fascinated by her explanation as to why we must never kill a spider.

There was once a beautiful Romany princess called Aranyi who boasted that she had been given by the gods the gift of making silk finer than the silkworm. She was told by a gipsy *choovahanee* that only one insect in the world was capable of that. The Princess was scornful, jeered at the witch, who then turned on her and told her that since she could spin more finely than the silkworm, and only the spider was capable of that, then she would be turned into a spider. No Romany, said Anyeta, would ever dare to kill a spider ever after and run the risk of bringing upon himself Aranyi's curse of evil.

Animals and insects occur in Romany legend and magic

and there are many superstitions surrounding these. I have
described how hotchi-witchi, the hedgehog, was a favourite
animal of mine. My very unfavourite is the weasel, an animal
the gipsies believe to be evil.

When a pregnant woman sees a weasel in her path she will
have ill luck brought to her unborn child, or he will be born
malformed, say the Romanies. Any gipsy caravan coming
across a weasel must change direction, or they will be in some
kind of trouble. Those who walk ahead or track the way, tie a
tuft of woman's hair to a branch near the spot where the
weasel was seen and then mark the way to go on the ground.
The way was marked for a change of direction by three lines,
one long and two short, once the weasel had been located. But
you must never kill a weasel, for the whole tribe will have bad
luck for a long time after.

Here are some of the other signs used by gipsies: a cross +
people here give nothing; a circle ○ generous people; a circle
with a dot inside ⊙ friendly to gipsies; an upright line crossed
by two lines ⧧ you'll not be welcomed here; a triangle △ you
can tell fortunes here; two wavy lines like the sea ≈ the
mistress desires a child; a triangle with one horizontal line △
the master died recently; a triangle with two horizontal lines
⧩ the mistress died recently; small 1 over a cross $\frac{1}{x}$ marriage
in the air.

13

Where do we come from?

When I asked Xavier. "Where do we come from?" I was not asking to be told the facts of life, as well he knew. Any child brought up in the countryside is well aware of how life begins. The knowledge comes naturally, right from one's early days. It seemed a commonplace, and was not worth serious discussion at the age of nine.

What I really wanted to know was where my people and his had sprung from. It was evident from the difference in our customs and those of the people in whose land we lived—and it was evident, too, in the attitude some of them took to us—that we were interlopers, that our backgrounds must be of extreme diversity.

I had been at school for over a year and I was not very welcome in some of the classrooms I attended, a fact I recognized quite early. It was not that I was dirty or stank, or that I was dark—for I was as fair as a Suffolk Dane or a Sussex Saxon, due to Marie's part in my ancestry—yet I could feel hostility from some of my classmates. It was mostly the boys who resented me.

"We come," said Xavier at last, in reply to my constant questioning, "from India. About nine hundred years ago it began, I think, for before that time there is no record of gipsies, as we are called, in Europe.

"Yes, the gipsies left India, we know not why, and dispersed over the face of the earth. They moved towards the setting sun, both to gain time on the duration of day and, too, on death.

"Through Afghanistan and Persia they came, reaching the Caspian Sea (to the north) of the Persian Gulf. They had split into different bands earlier. The northern tribe crossed Armenia to the Caucasus and later Russia; the southern tribe went up the Euphrates and Tigris."

"Where is Afghanistan and Persia and the Euphrates?" I asked.

"Look on the schoolroom map," said Xavier, and I couldn't tell whether he himself knew or not.

"Then some went to the Black Sea and others to Syria, but the majority went to Turkey. Another tribe went through Palestine and Egypt.

"This southern group went along the north African coast until they came to Gibraltar and crossed into Spain and these, Lion, are our cousins the Gitanos. The branch from which we come had passed through Turkey, crossed the Bosporus, into Greece and the Balkans, and from there into Central Europe.

"Now," said Xavier, "this is what I learnt from a very clever gentleman, an admiral who had made a study of our history, and I believe him. But Anyeta will tell you this—and it is the traditional legend of our beginnings:

"There are two peoples who were the original gipsies. The *Gond*, of Nepal and Burma, and the *Sinti*, who came out of India, crossed the frontier and became horse-breakers. They it was who taught the Chaldeans, the people whose land they reached by caravan—trading in gems, working skilfully in bronze and gold—they taught these people yoga, how to walk through fire, and the art of tumbling. And in exchange they were taught the local art of astrology. And all this happened before the days of Abraham.

"Later the *Sinti* left Chaldea and turned towards Egypt and impressed the Pharaohs with their feats and so won their right to stay in that country. And that is how we came to be called gipsies, for it was believed that we had come out of Egypt when we crossed to Europe and the Europeans named us after the word 'Egyptian'.

"Now," said Xavier, drawing a chart for me, "there are three main groups of gipsies. The *Kalderash*, who are tin-smiths and copper-smiths, and they come from Central Europe. And among them are the *Lovari* who came originally from Hungary, and I am from this group because I have Hungarian gipsy blood. The *Boyhas* from Transylvania went mainly to France and are renowned for their performing animals. The *Luri Tschurari*, another group, live apart from others of the *Kalderash* group.

"The second main group, the *Gitanos*, live in Spain, Portugal and the South of France," said Xavier.

"And the third group is the *Manush* whose name means 'true men' in Sanskrit. They are called *Sinti* because they come from India on the banks of the Sind. Of these the *Valsikanes* are travelling showmen and circus folk. The *Gaygikanes* live in Germany and the *Piemontesi* are in Italy.

"In this country the gipsies are linked to the *Kalderash* and *Manush* people."

He was brief in his instruction, for he was never one to dwell in the past, but always looking to the future. His antecedents did not bother him one way or the other; he knew who he was, the knowledge gave him dignity, and that was the end of it. He was a man prepared to move with the times, and was very modern in outlook, more from expediency than any other qualities, I suppose.

In later years I determined to find out more about our origins, and spent some time reading in public libraries, making notes and delving into the fascinating history of my people.

From 1417 onwards there are many reports of the gipsy visitation to Europe, with a follow-up in about 1438. The early visit in 1417 was by a mere three hundred families, who were probably part of a reconnaissance party. The sea journey to Britain must have been quite difficult for them to undertake, for it is known that gipsies hate the water (although it plays a part in our rituals) and although they would traverse wide deserts and mountains even, they were in great fear of crossing the seas.

This early band's visitation has been chronicled quite minutely. From Lüneburg in Germany they went on to Lübeck and Rostock. There were reports of them being great thieves, especially the women. In 1418 they had reached Leipzig and Frankfurt am Main, then they went to Zürich, Basle, and Berne in Switzerland.

By 1422 they were in Bologna and on the road to Rome. And by 1427 they were at the gates of Paris.

Who were this original band? The German chroniclers said they looked like Tartars, for they still remembered invasions by the Vandals. These new invaders were dark-skinned people who advanced in long caravans, some on foot and some on horseback, drawing waggons of baggage, and full of women and children, but however fierce they may have appeared, they claimed in truth to be good Christians.

Their story was that their return to paganism from the Christian faith after their first conversion had caused their wandering life. The bishops had given them a penance: they must wander abroad for seven years. They showed 'Letters of Protection' from rulers such as Sigismund, King of the Romans, which got them an 'in' with snobs!

The letter of protection was impressive:

"We, Sigismund . . . King of Hungary, Bohemia, Dalmatia, Croatia and of other places . . . Our faithful Ladislas, Voivode of the Gypsies and others dependent on him have humbly besought Us to bear witness of our special

My nation-wide star-gazing days began at *Woman's Own* in 1957 when
I took over the astrology column after my father's death

My father in his Romany togs with his faithful friend

benevolence. It has pleased Us to receive their compliant request and not to refuse them this present letter. In consequence, if the aforesaid Ladislas and his people present themselves in any place within Our Empire, town or village, we enjoin you to show your loyalty towards Us. You will protect them in every way, so that the Voivode Ladislas and the Gypsies his subjects can reside within your walls. If there should be found among them some drunken woman, if any troublesome incident should occur among them, no matter what its nature, it is Our will and formal command that the said Voivode Ladislas and he alone shall then use the right to punish and to absolve, to the exclusion of you all."

This impressive letter was naturally a very good way in, but the 'Egyptians' did not, unfortunately, keep their side of the bargain—for surely safe conduct should be repaid by good conduct—and in 1422 when one chief named Michael of Egypt led his group to Italy and Bologna, a historian of the day records:

"Many people went very respectfully to find Duke Michael's wife to have their future told by her, and so in actual fact many things happened, some learning what would be their lot, none in any case returning without having their purse or some item of clothing stolen. The women of those people went through the town between six and eight o'clock, displayed their talents in the houses of burghers, seizing everything upon which they could lay their hands. Others went into shops as if to make purchases, but in fact to steal. Throughout the whole of Bologna there was petty thieving on a vast scale. As a result of this it was proclaimed that a fine of fifty livres would be imposed on whoever engaged in any business with those foreigners, as well as excommunication . . .

"These vagabonds are the cleverest thieves in the world. When there was nothing more to be stolen, they left for Rome."

And good riddance!

By 1430 gipsies had reached England, but nobody seems to know how we crossed the Channel. It's thought we came from the mouth of the Elbe.

The first official reference to the newcomers is in Scotland in 1449 and contained in an Act of Scottish Parliament directed against "sorners, overliers, and masterful beggars, with horse, hounds or other goods". Sorners were people who forcibly quartered themselves on others. Although there is no mention of 'Egyptians' in this Act, there's little doubt it was aimed at the gipsies.

The first reference to gipsies as such occurs in 1505, April 22nd: "Item to the Egyptians," writes the Lord High Treasurer at the Court of King James of Scotland, "be the king's command vii lib." Seven pounds—probably for some kind of entertainment.

Gipsies seemed to have reached my home county of Suffolk in 1520, for there is a record of 'Gipsions' entertained by the Earl of Surrey at Tendring Hall, and in 1521 William Cholomely gave certain 'Egyptians' at Thornbury forty shillings.

From this time on gipsies are mentioned more and more frequently in English country records.

They did not make themselves popular. Henry VIII took severe measures to meet their misdeeds. And Elizabeth I was even more severe, accusing them of hiding priests and emissaries of Rome. In 1563 she commanded them to leave the country or within three months there would be the penalty of death; an enormous task, for at that time there were estimated to be ten thousand gipsies in the realm. However, they managed to survive and regained their freedom in the seventeenth century.

In 1530 an act had been passed 'from henceforth no such Psone be suffred to come within this Kynge's Realme', which must have been the work of some sixteenth-century Fascist, perhaps. Just to be a gipsy was enough to bring sentence of death, but the measures were evidently not effective. The last recorded death sentence was carried out in Cromwell's time at the Suffolk assize, when thirteen gipsies were hung.

There are records of gipsies' children being baptized in English churches as far back as the sixteenth century.

As life became safer and measures became less stern the British gipsies settled down, formed tribes and elected chiefs; one of the most famous of these was James Bosvill (or Boswell), buried at Doncaster.

The gipsies of Wales are said to have been the most faithful to old traditions. They are the only gipsies in the world to this day to use the language *Romany* in its pure state. The rest use a certain amount of *kant* and *didikai* slang as well. My father always called himself a 'Romany' rather than a 'Gipsy' because he wished to identify with the language and his Welsh antecedents, although in fact, there is no such division of the race.

Borrow was the first man to live in Britain with the Romany-speaking gipsies and learn their ways and their language.

I completed my education about my people by reading those two classics *The Romany Rye* and *Lavengro* by George Borrow.

Borrow came from Norwich and at the early age of fourteen was already loitering about those parts of the town frequented by wanderers, foreigners and gipsy horse dealers. On Mousehold Heath he lived with the gipsies in their encampments and went inside their tents—a rare occurrence for a *gorgio*.

He stained his face with walnuts and lived with his new friends in dens in the hillsides. From them he learnt the Romany language, presumably an easy task for at sixteen he was already a scholar of Welsh, Danish, Arabic and Hebrew.

In 1825 he bought a donkey and cart and set out from London to walk across England; he earned his keep as a tin-smith, but was for this reason up against a few gipsies on the way, because they were understandably jealous of his com-petition. Later he worked his way across France and southern Europe and travelled as far as Russia by selling Bibles door to door.

Borrow lived for five years in Spain and in 1841 published *The Zincali*—a work about the Spanish Gitanos. Later he wrote his two great romantic works, *Lavengro* and *The Romany Rye*. He is our most important source of information about European gipsies.

So, these are the bones of the matter, there is a long tradition of legend and truth intermingled concerning our beginnings. I believe I have set it out fairly simply here.

Where do we come from? The answer is from a source which started off as a trickle, became a stream, then a tributary and finally a great river rushing out of India and flooding all Europe throughout the fifteenth and sixteenth centuries, until Scandinavia (in the seventeenth century) and North America (in the nineteenth century) had been reached.

Nothing, it seems, could dam this tidal rush, not even sentence of death, ostracism, hatred nor acrimony. The gipsy today is threatened in these islands by modern 'civilization'. My father could see it coming years ago and was philo-sophical about it.

"Time to get out of the vardo soon and off the road, Lion," he said. "The quality of life for us *Roms* will only get worse if we try to fight what is happening."

Xavier even opened a bank account in the end, forsaking the wicker strong-box and two Alsatian hounds he had latterly kept, for stronger bars and locks. Because in those days there was no Capital Gains Tax, he didn't have to explain his hoard of bank notes. He disapproved of Income Tax, but he was not alone in this.

It was his signal, when he walked through the doors of the National Provincial Bank in Colchester, that the old days had gone for ever.

14

Curse of the Romanies

As I grew up within the charmed circle of Xavier, Marie and Anyeta, my ears stuffed with good advice, fairy tales, folklore and admonition of varying degrees according to my behaviour, one very significant fact of the Romany life blazoned itself on my consciousness: the Romany curse. It dawned on me gradually, little by little, that people—that is, *gorgios*—were actually afraid of it and its effect on their lives. They believed in it, and so in the end did I, for it's true I had heard many a tale from Anyeta's lips about curses coming true, even after several years.

Nowadays, with some knowledge of how a witch-doctor works in Africa, or even how a bully operates in a working situation or within a family, I know that self-suggestion has a great part to play. But then, surrounded as I was by the lore and magic of whispered, half-heard recountings of curses long ago that worked their dreadful fate, I believed. Oh, I believed.

Xavier used to tell me that he had more requests by husbands and wives than he could count on the fingers of both hands, to place a curse on an unfortunate spouse. Did he ever do it? I asked him.

He pulled his moustache, shook his head then laughed. "Why, boy, I do remember once I gave way to temptation and advised a woman how she could lay a curse on her husband

and kill him without the police being any the wiser.

"She had come to me and told me a tale of how she hated her man and she had prayed for him to die, but no one seemed interested in her prayers as they had been going on for some time and there he was, alive as ever.

"She was a huge woman, terrifying, with a face like the back of a bus, and I had seen the husband she wanted so much out of the way. He was a poor, thin little man with a melancholy face and a weedy moustache.

"Well, I told this stupid *gorgio* that there was one spell that could not fail, but she, too, must play her part. She begged me to go on and was all ears. I told her that she must give him a beef-steak pudding every day, help him to a good portion of it, and see that he ate every mouthful. I told her that this would give him the most terrible pains and eventually kill him through causing the heart to cease to work through its rolls of encircling fat, to say nothing of the spell I would cast over his plate.

"And I told her, Lion, that on the strength of this curse he could not last out a year, but that lest he suspect her intent the dish was to be varied occasionally with other meats. I said that the curses of Romanies work far more quickly if the women using them speak less. I told her to talk to her husband less and to be polite to him. She promised that she would and went away to do her worst."

Xavier chuckled. "Two months later I was passing their cottage and there he was in the garden, looking as if he found life very pleasant. He had brightened up and put on flesh. Poor old man, he was having his first decent meals, and in blissful silence, in all his married life. I didn't stay around too long after that, boy, to find out if my curse worked or not. But he must have died a happy man."

Part of the Romany reluctance during the past few hundred years to place curses is the infiltration of Christianity—a religion that has taken hold of their hearts and imaginations.

But I remember the day Anyeta told me of another religion long ago and of the beginning of the world.

"Once, Romany *chal*, there was nothing, there was nothing within nothing," said Anyeta, describing two circles in the air within one another. "And inside the smallest," I suppose she meant void, "there was the sleeping god. And the god began to dream and from this dream came many small sparks which joined together in a big ball of fire, white hot it was, *chal*, and then it became so hot that it did explode and flew out in all directions. It was of many little bits, and these cooled as they flew. And these are the stars and the sun and the moon and the earth.

"And when the great explosion came two gods were born: Moshto, the god of Life, and Arivell, the god of Death. And Moshto had three sons. The eldest went on creating life, and the second mended what had to be mended, and the third destroyed all that was bad or beyond hope. And the most important of these was the second son."

"Why?" I asked, but she couldn't tell me.

"It is so," she said. "Then, *chal*, the devil made two statues of clay, but they were lifeless until the god Moshto breathed life into them with the seeds of the Ginko tree which he blew into their mouths. And as they awoke they stood in front of two fruit trees, an apple tree in front of the woman, and a pear tree in front of the man. And the woman ate the apple, and the man ate the pear and they called these the fruits of knowledge; but they had been put there by Arivell, the devil. And they had lost the everlasting life by eating the fruits, but they multiplied and they farmed the land to the far corners of the earth and it is from them that we come, *chal*."

Later, when I first heard the story of Adam and Eve at a village school in Essex, I was tempted to interrupt and say that it was right in the main, but that they had got their details wrong. However, I thought better of it. And for many years after I was totally confused in my young mind as to which was the real truth. Still, I suppose that one version is as valid as the other, in the sense that both are beautiful allegories.

It was Moshto, god of Life and not Arivell, god of Death, who had created disease, Anyeta told me. Moshto, it seemed, had created a race of good fairies to protect and help man, and these fairies had a beautiful queen who lived in a crystal palace on a mountaintop. Not to be outdone, Arivell had created a demon people who lived under the mountain itself and came out only on very dark nights.

One night the king of the demons went up to introduce himself to the beautiful queen and propose marriage, said Anyeta, because he wanted to rule not only her but also her people. And when she saw him she was so appalled at his appearance that she swooned. While she was unconscious, the demon king found a secret passage from the mountain to the castle and let in all his demon people; this evil horde then proceeded to kill and eat many of the fairies. When the queen came to she gave way and agreed to marry the demon king in order to stop this terrible cannibalism, and she bore him demon children more vile and repulsive than he was himself.

Anyeta here recited a long list of names. These were the spreaders of disease; one child of this unhappy coupling spread the plague, another dysentery, or another merely a head as thick as a plank. The catarrh demon was especially hideous, for he had the head of a man and the body of a fish and as he went past you the nine long sticky hairs on each cheek would pierce you and give you catarrh. So said Anyeta.

I was not quite sure whether to believe all this, for I was not a child troubled by nightmares and had never seen or experienced anything unpleasant, except perhaps the killing of animals, which was all part of the way of life in the country, so that I had grown up in a sunny country of the mind, free from fear of bogey men and unacquainted with Grimm's fairy-tales. It seemed to me Anyeta was talking nonsense, but

I didn't tell her so, nor did I go to Xavier for confirmation or contradiction.

I only uttered a curse once; it was not premeditated, but spontaneous. I shall never do it again, for it was a shock to me as much as to anyone else that it appeared to work.

It happened during my raw 'rookie' days in His Majesty's Service at a Somerset station where we began our training with footslogging and drill. I had joined up and been accepted, ear-ring, long hair and all, for recruitment in the RAF—I was determined this was to be my Service, for like all young men in those days I wanted to fly.

The Guards or any other branch of the army would never have taken me, with my long red locks and my gold sleepers— in any case, I never gave them a chance. But the RAF accepted my long hair (at least it was long by the standards of those days), and there would be no problem if I was intended for air crew, as many military-type rules were relaxed for them.

My fellow rookies accepted me as I was—or perhaps they felt that at twelve stone, with broad shoulders and nearly six feet tall, I was not worth tackling! It was evident that I could easily hold my own in a fracas. But there was a corporal who shall be nameless who hated me on sight.

Day after day on the barrack square he taunted me and jibed at me. It was not the usual 'you 'orrible little man' type of sneer that traditional sergeant majors use as a jibe to enliven somnolent rookies. No, this was aimed not only at me, personally, but at my whole race.

"Come along Gippo, get those shoulders back. Though how you expect to look smart with all that golden goldilocks 'anging on yer collar I'll never know."

"Pick up yer feet, you crummy gippo, anyone'd think you were a girl, poncing around with those ear-rings."

Day after day the jeers rolled from his thin lips. He was a little man, dark, with short back and sides; a man whose forage-cap did nothing for his rather bleak features and large, hairy ears. Meeting as equals on a dark night he would never have dared to needle me like that, my long melford was still my best punch! But here, on the parade ground and on route marches, he was safe, with his two stripes up, from retaliation.

One day, unhappily for him, he went too far. He didn't shout, but came up to me and sticking his long nose in my face—or round about the area of my neck—and peering into my eyes, he said: "Pity Hitler doesn't get rid of you lot in this war—if he did that the little bastard would have done some good."

I could hardly believe my ears. Nor could the men standing either side of me, because I could sense their unease. Immediately I let rip the most sacred and terrible words of the Romany curse. I would rather have hit him, but that would have meant being put on a charge.

He was startled, turned pale, almost spat in my face as he told me that I was going to be put on a charge the next time I did anything like that, but, for some reason, either a feeling of shame that he had taunted me like that, or a fear of the words he didn't understand, he let me off this time.

On the march along the country road I regretted my outburst and tried to remember how to reverse the curse. A squad was approaching from the other direction, under the command of another NCO, marching, as we were, at ease. The corporal ran across to speak to his brother officer, but omitted to look both ways on that quiet road, and incredibly, for no one understood quite how it happened, he was run down by the local bus. He spent a long time in hospital, and my fellow rookies treated me with even more respect from then on. Luckily, I was moved to training farther afield—in Canada—before the aggressive little man was out of hospital.

To this day I can't make up my mind whether it was in his stars that such a thing would happen on that day, or whether it was my curse that worked the deed. Anyway, you may rest assured that I have never repeated the curse, and am never likely to.

Many people have asked me if I can reverse a curse. The answer, according to lore, is yes, but I have never encouraged anyone to think that they have been the subject of a curse, even though a number of women have come to me with tales of gipsy women at the door who left a curse on them for not buying or responding to their begging. I always say that such a curse would not work, for no true Romany would curse anyone for not responding to a plea for the sale of goods—it is up to him or her to be skilful enough in the sales patter to persuade a sale every time. As for begging, that, according to my father's tribe, was not the way of true Roms.

It has always been part of our lore that bread and grain are the antidote to evil, to witches, to spells and bad luck generally, even against the devil. Some gipsies sew bread inside their horses' collars to protect them from 'witching'. I confess now that I often carry a lump of bread in my pocket for luck. There have been thousands of Romanies down the centuries who have believed in the magic of grain, and even today some are never without some wheat about their person.

"The good God's grain" was how Anyeta always talked of it, and she told me that if I were chased by the *beng* (devil) or a *mulo* (demon) then I should run straight for the cornfield and hide there for safety, and the pursuer would disappear.

Happy days. If only that would work with the tax inspector.

15

The Big-Time

I always remember the day Rufus was sniffing round a basket
in the market at Colchester.

"Hey, you, dog, get out of it!" The shout came from a huge
man whose property the basket appeared to be. Inflamed with
rage, he gave the dog a kick that sent it hurtling along the
street. Xavier wasted no time, but strode up to the molester—
who was several inches taller than himself, a real lout—
grabbed his nose between finger and thumb and twisted it till
the victim's eyes watered. His opponent was helpless. I
watched, holding my breath and stroking down Rufus's ruffled
fur, while the man howled his protest.

A crowd gathered. "Serve you right, you cowardly bully,"
growled Xavier giving the startled man a wallop on the jaw
from which he went reeling, then turned on his heel and
marched off down the centre lane of the stalls to a respectful
hush. He was not followed. In those days they seldom called
the police to sort out a disagreement or a fight. It was just one
of those things; you had to look after yourself.

I had been taught early in life to use my fists, but lectured
on the value of control by Xavier. He was not very controlled
himself, and was easily upset, but he was careful to warn me
off impulsive outbursts. My mother, too, not at all happy
about the prospect of having her son's handsome features
ruined, later blocked my way into professional boxing which
Xavier was eager for me to take up!

Xavier, however, did not heed his own warnings, and treated fighting as a hobby. Many's the time he would be found slogging it out in a meadow with a willing opponent. His most enthusiastic audience was usually composed of a few yokels and me. It was not thought to be 'violence' in those days, people were merely more inclined to work their aggressions out of their system by a very natural outlet, I think.

I spent some of my time fighting village boys, and winning, so that after the first encounter they were usually scared or respectful of me.

Xavier told me that he taught the Chelmsford Police wrestling, another of his favourite sports, but I have no proof that this was the truth.

There were times when he'd set up a ring in a village square, challenge the local lads to come and fight him for a prize of money, and charge the onlookers a penny a time to watch the show! He was careful to inflict the minimum of damage and, of course, there were always the times when he was prepared to suffer defeat, if only to give the next challenger a false sense of confidence.

My pre-occupation with professional fights became almost as obsessional as my love of the theatres, the Palaces of Variety I visited as soon as I could pay the price of admission.

The magic of show business has always been a strong lure; as a young *chal* I had often been taken to a music hall show by Xavier, so it was natural that when I was older I should continue to go by myself.

During these performances, witnessed mainly from the 'gods' at sixpence a time, the acts would come on in no particular order. The programme gave each 'turn' a number and a young lady would walk onto the stage bearing a card which showed the number of the next one, so that if you referred to your printed programme you could see what was to ravish your senses next . . . the Spider's Web—a fantasy dance, the Juggling Brothers from Romania, or Miss Lottie with the slightly blue songs.

When I was young, Xavier used to take me to lovely pantomimes, 'Babes in the Wood' and 'Red Riding Hood'. My father was stage-struck, and, if we were staying on the outskirts of a town, Ipswich, Norwich, Cambridge, Crewe, he'd make straight for the theatre in the evenings where he'd go backstage and make himself known to the cast. He would always go round to the pub frequented by the performers, and he would often help to shift scenery (no unions to object in those days, but in any case he would do this free of charge) so in love was he with the atmosphere.

The day Xavier came home with a huge sack of sugar that he'd got for a few pence, being short of money I devised the idea of paying for my ticket in a different currency than money. I gave the man at the door of the Hippodrome, Crewe, a bag of sugar and he was delighted.

There were times, too, when I'd joined Xavier in his stage management ventures. At King's Lynn they were doing 'East Lynn', and it was my job to toll the bell when little Willie was dying. I was also engaged to turn a big wheel of a drum to make wind, or rattle a sheet of corrugated iron to create the noise of thunder. I loved doing this so much I wouldn't stop when I was supposed to.

Very often the only entertainment available in the provincial towns, these shows certainly fell short of the glamorous standards of today, but to me they were pure enchantment, and I revelled in them. While other kids were at the cinema, I would seek out the town's Music Hall or the Pierrot Show on the pier and sit there wrapt, consumed, thrilled, too, by everything I saw and heard. I was no mean dancer, myself, though I hadn't always enjoyed my father's efforts to teach me clog dancing, and sometimes felt a bit of a *dindilo* when he later presented it as one of the turns with his travelling band of 'gipsies'.

The Petulengro Gipsy Band may well be remembered by some of you. It was formed in the thirties and was going strong during the Second World War. It grew in size and in its skills and toured the country with great success, but behind-scenes it was never free of squabbles, jealousies and fights. I don't know how my father coped with all this, except to say that he was at first both a strong and a good-humoured man, though he later changed.

Never very lucky in love in those early days, I immediately fell for a beautiful young trapeze artiste who joined the company in the double-act with a slightly older man whom I in my innocence took to be her father. It was only when Xavier took me aside and made me promise to stop pestering her with my attentions or else—that I was grieved and shocked to realize the 'elderly' man was, in fact, her lover. A late starter in some ways, I began to learn very quickly about life from my showbiz colleagues.

The Band of Players numbered seven. There were seven instrumentalists, but my father, being artful, found out that if he could produce eight he would be paid a bigger fee by the theatre management. So I was taught mime (my playing never having been up to standard). I sat there happily sawing away in silence while the others around me produced the vital sound and Xavier was able to collect his larger fee.

I was also taught a dance routine with a member of the company, a girl dressed as a gipsy. I'd rush onto the stage from the side, meet her almost head on, we'd crash tam-bourines, knock knees and arms, throw the tambourines away and do a dance; then I was supposed to take her in my arms and jump over a camp fire at the side of the stage. A typical Romany wedding, Xavier would tell the audience. I was sixteen, but strong for my age!

All went well until we reached the Argyll, Birkenhead. The stage was small and because I knew the dance so well I hadn't bothered to rehearse. I knew it so well I'd sing the tune in my

Today I live in a house and travel by car, not in the vardo – but I am still happiest in the country

Woman's Own astrological 'phone-in' turned out to be one of the most popular ever.

sleep; I was getting bored with the same old routine.

At the first performance at Birkenhead, I didn't allow for the size of the stage, and feeling particularly strong almost threw my partner into the nearest box. Xavier was not pleased and told me so with the help of a cuff round the ears. At sixteen I felt this to be undignified, and began to brood on the nature of my life now. But I was by no means unhappy.

The band toured the north in those days a good deal and when I joined it as a sort of silent fiddler and dancer extraordinary, I began to learn a good deal, too, about the circuit of theatrical landladies.

As is often the custom among younger, poorer members of a company, I shared a bedroom with a violinist called Heinrik —a pleasant change from sharing with my father, who had been my room-mate in the first few weeks of touring. The only advantage of this arrangement had been that he was a heavy man, slept soundly, and so I was able to press my narrow dancing trousers under his mattress. Heinrik was a far lighter man, skin and bone in fact, so my trews stayed rather less well pressed. However, we were nearer in age and had a good deal of fun together.

Looking back we did some disgraceful things to landladies who had, by their rules and sanctions, given us a hard time. At one harridan's place we decided to cut a bobble a day from the fancy braid over the mantelpiece; there were quite a few bobbles missing when the company moved on. I frequently used to wonder if she ever solved the mystery.

At another 'digs' we nailed a kipper behind the wardrobe; it was a particularly dirty digs that had never been cleaned during our whole stay there. At another set of digs we broke a chair and stuck it together with HP Sauce. Such childishness probably does us no credit, yet it was light relief to us from the heavy discipline of my father's company. He would never stand any nonsense and didn't allow any of us to drink or smoke. He may have been wise in his way, but he was only able to carry out these rules by force of personality, and with me, a certain amount of bullying.

Our relationship began to change; the 'lion' was growing up and beginning to want to stretch his limbs, walk out of the over-protective shadow. But Xavier still looked on me as a boy, and it began to occur to me that I could even be looked on as a rival; after all I had the same name. His overbearing ways started to annoy me more and more.

"Do this, Lion; go there; carry this; move that; change the set; it's badly timed that dance of yours, practise it."

Slowly before my eyes he changed from the genial, protective, father figure to a bossy and grumpy tyrant.

He began telling me when to get back to digs, which girls not to take out. After a year of touring I asked for more money—as a member of the family I was paid least—two pounds a week. To make things worse, Marie had decided to stay at home for most of the time. Taking her home with her on the *drom* was one thing; leaving it and travelling the north and forever waiting on Crewe Station on wet Sundays was not her idea of a happy life. My father and I saw her about one weekend in four.

The crunch came for the Romany Boy when Heinrik and I inadvertently set the 'camp fire' alight (it was a brilliant piece of faking, a red electric light bulb covered by a grid of sticks on which was artistically arranged curls of flame-coloured paper). As the conflagration went up and the safety curtain came down, we collapsed with helpless waves of shuddering laughter at the absurdity of it all. Xavier did not think it was funny. In fact, he blew his top, placing most of the blame on his son.

"*Dindilo*," he roared, "you've ruined the show." He put up his fists and came at me there and then for a fight.

I had been taught well, but he had not taught me well enough—besides, he was much heavier than me, several stones. By the time my nose began bleeding he had stopped, taking it for granted that the fight was his. By this time the stage-hands had doused the small fire, the curtain went up, but the audience, very naturally, had gone. We stood staring out at an empty auditorium.

Like most fights in the Romany world, this one was soon forgotten by Xavier, but not by me. I was starting to question his authority. I no longer accepted his sanctions, I was beginning to find him old-fashioned, overbearing, and could sense a danger to my own development. At seventeen I decided I'd had enough.

"I'm starting on my own," I told him.

He laughed. "What are you on about now? You haven't got the guts, you *bilaco*. You're good for nothing but *tatting* rags and bottles. *Scarper*. I haven't got time to waste on you."

He appeared to be a completely changed man. Either the worries of running the company were too much for him, or the applause of the audience had gone to his head. I wandered away hunch-shouldered to talk it over with Heinrik, who agreed that my best course was to *scarper*, to take his orders literally, and go away.

There being no time like the present, I packed all I had, took my *bunce* for the past few weeks from under the mattress and caught the train north to Blackpool. Heinrik was sworn to secrecy about my direction. As the train pulled out of Preston I was still depressed and miserable. Doubt began to spread through my mind as to whether I was doing the right thing. I had no money or possessions beyond what was packed in my battered suitcase. My father was slowly but surely becoming a rich man, but he had not passed any of his wealth on to me in the slightest degree. But I had my wits, my health and my crystal ball. I was after all a Romany with a knowledge of astrology, palmistry, the whole gamut of fortune-telling, and if anyone would welcome me it would be the ladies of Blackpool.

I opened the window and looked out to the West, fancying I could smell sea air. It was going to be all right and I silently wished myself *kooshti bok*.

Glossary

N.B. *Although this glossary is for the most part comprised of Romany words, there are also a certain number of 'Kant' and 'Slang' words. These are marked with a 'K' and 'S' respectively.*

atchen tan: stopping place
av akai: come here

bakalo: lucky
baulo cirol: pig roasting
beng: devil
bikin: to sell
bilaco: good-for-nothing, idiot
blistering moosh: magistrate (K)
bok: luck
boreen: lane
boro: great, big
bosa-veno: fiddler
bosh: fiddle (K)
bunce: profit (K)

caneegra: hare
cane-fakir: mender of cane-
    seated chairs
cannie: chicken
chal: boy
chav: child, term of endearment

chavis: children
cherino: star
chi: girl
chingary: commotion, fight
chiv barrer: knife/scissor
    grinder (K)
chop: to barter (K)
chorar: to steal
chumeidai: sacred kiss of
    marriage
coor: to strike, hit
coor the drom: hit the road

dands: teeth (K)
didikai: not a pure Romany
dindilo: idiot
dinlo: silly
divvas: day
dloova: money
dordi, dordi: Romany words of
    exclamation (e.g. alas,
    alack! goodness me! etc.)

drabengro: poison-maker, chemist
drom: road
dukkerin: hand-reading
Duvel: God

engala: cuddle
engro: maker

faida: pegs
filisin: mansion

gavaste: town
gavvers: police (K)
gillie: song
givengro: farmer
gorgio: non-gipsy
grafting: working (S)
grunter: pig (S)
grye: horse
grye-kuper: horse-dealer
gurni: cow (K)

habben: feast, food
hotchi-witchi: hedgehog

jal avree: go away
jinnick: donkey
joovi: woman
joskin: farm labourer (S)
juggal: dog
juval: woman

kaba: kettle
kant: didikai language
kaulochirilo: blackbird
kini: gipsy wine
kip: bed (K)

kooshti: good
kor: to fight
kosh: wood, stick

lil: book
lulagi: flower
luller: arrest (K)

makadi: dirty, impure
matchi: fish (K)
maulie: fist
merno: mine
meski: tea
mokadi jook: fox
monisha: wife (K)
moocher: beggar (K)
moon: month (K)
moosh: man
mug-fakir: photographer (K)
mulled-moosh-engro: doctor (dead man maker)
mulo: demon
mumper: tramp (K)
mumpli: the ways of a mumper
mush: umbrella (K)
mush-fakir: maker or mender of umbrellas (K)

nafli: ill
nanti: not, never
narked: bad, dark
nav: name

odjus: beautiful, lovely

parni: rain, water
parni-kip-lulagi: dandelion (*lit.* piddle-bed-flower)

pateran: design, trail
patrin: leaf
pattriensis: herbs
petul: horseshoe
pikey: umbrella (S)
pikie: a gipsy who has been
  expelled from his tribe
plastramengro: peace-maker,
  policeman
pooker: tell
poori: old
poshrat: half-breed
pral: brother
puridaia: grandmother
purum: onion
puvengra: potato

raklo: girl
rokker: speak, talk
rom: man
rommer: marry
rommerin: wedding
roy: prince
rye: gentleman

sante: health
scarper: go away, run away (S)

shallow-runner: tramp who
  deliberately goes around
  looking unkempt, in tatters
  (S)
shooshie: rabbit (K)
shoovani: witch

tan: tent
tarno: little, young
taso-fakir: china-mender
tatting: collecting (S)
tattitatti: baked potato (K)
tikner: baby
tog-fencer: market worker who
  sells clothes (S)
togs: clothes (S)

vardo: caravan, waggon

wafodi: bad, wicked
weshengro: gamekeeper
wongur: money

yag: fire
yagged: burned

Index

tribal lore, customs and
  legends, 21-2, 24-8, 117-24
Turkey, 126

umbrella-mender, 101

Valsikanes, The, 127
vardo, the, 12, 13, 14, 15, 16

Wales, 12, 131
Wackett, Miss, 28

Water Street, 111
Waveney, River, 87
West Mersea, 114
Wolsey, Cardinal, 110
Woodford, 41

Zig, 56
Zincali, The (book), 132
Zingaris, 57, 72, 75
Zurich, 128